"We have a poster at our company that reads 'The systems you have in place are perfectly organized to produce the behaviors you are currently experiencing.' If you are seeking new behaviors and better results, new systems are the only way to get there. *Creating an Effective Management System* is just the book to get you started. The decades of experience-based wisdom that Graupp, Steward and Parsons share will set you on a new path to a more joyful organization and the tangible results it will produce."

– Rich Sheridan, CEO, Menlo Innovations; author of *Joy, Inc.* and *Chief Joy Officer*

"A fine book by skilled practitioners that integrates Kata and TWI, with Strategy Deployment in pursuit of an integrated management system. Well done, Skip, Brad and Patrick."

– Pascal Dennis, president, Lean Pathways Inc.; author of *Lean Production Simplified, Andy & Me, Andy & Me and the Hospital, Getting the Right Things Done, and The Remedy*

"Systems thinking is, and always has been, a rare commodity in management. It is what separates the ultra-high-performers from the rest. In this practical and engaging book, Patrick Graupp, Skip Steward, and Brad Parsons give a concise and extremely clear explanation of what systems thinking looks like in a healthcare setting. And they do so in a way that translates easily to any type of organization. Highly recommended!"

– Alan Robinson, co-author of *Ideas Are Free* and *The Idea-Driven Organization*

"Patrick Graupp, writing with co-authors has produced an excellent series of books on TWI. This book is no exception. Although generally relevant, the first part of the book is written around hospitals. As such it is a very good introduction to Lean in hospitals, superior to all hospital-focused texts that I know of in the area. It makes use of a combination of a gear-train analogy of Lean systems together with the TWI 'three-legged stool' and policy deployment to give concise and practical guidance to hospital administrators, doctors and nurses."

– John Bicheno, Professor of Lean Enterprise, University of Buckingham

"Patrick Graupp, Skip Steward and Brad Parsons put into context the synergistic relationship between the Toyota Kata patterns that drive continuous improvement, and TWI skills that are essential along the way. The practical nature of the content makes this book a must for any leader working in any organization in any service or industry. Patrick is perhaps the best qualified person in the world in combining the theory of the TWI methods with practical application. Skip has been the driver of merging the skills and the Toyota Kata patterns supported along the way by Brad Parsons. Could the combination of Pat, Skip and Brad be any better for all our benefit?"

– Oscar Roche, Director, TWI Institute Australia and New Zealand

"Where most books only discuss the successful end state, Patrick, Skip, and Brad describe a system that emerges organically as the various pieces began interacting with one another. In doing so they give us a rare insight into how systems that work actually develop - not as something deliberately engineered and then implemented, but through shepherding the process of learning."

– Mark Rosenthal, blogger, theleanthinker.com; Principal, Novayama LLC

"If you are striving to provide an amazing patient experience, eliminate preventable harm, or improve health care outcomes, you must eventually examine your Management System. Your Management System must be capable of improving the work and sustaining those improvements. Graupp, Steward, and Parsons have captured the essence of how improvement in healthcare can be both achieved and sustained. The authors will challenge you to reflect on your own Management System as you strive towards excellence."

– Charles V. Hagood, DSc, President, Transformational
Advisory Services, Press Ganey Associates, Inc

"Creating an Effective Management System: Integrating Policy Deployment, TWI, and Kata is insightful – It challenges us to develop management systems where components need to work well together while building strong human relationships. Like the fact the authors explore in greater detail how well PD, TWI and Kata interact with each other. From personal experience, every management system must have these three basic components in order to be effective."

– Frank Gorena, Director of Operational Excellence, Interiors, Collins Aerospace

"In their wonderful new book, Graupp, Steward, and Parsons have put people where they belong: front and center. It's the perfect antidote to the mass of tools-focused continuous improvement advice."

– Dan Markovitz, Markovitz Consulting, author of A *Factory of One*

"The authors brilliantly illustrate, through numerous examples, how the strength of a management system resides in the understanding of how its key elements work together. Then, how organizations connect the dots and play the game becomes key to sustainable performance improvement."

– Sylvain Landry, Professor and Associate Director,
Healthcare Management Hub, HEC Montréal.

"When Kata was first introduced ten years ago it was very apparent that the power of the combination of the practice and skills of TWI and Kata could be a game changer. Graupp, Steward, and Parsons explain their groundbreaking work and story of accomplishing this in the arena of lean management."

– Jim Huntzinger, President and Founder, Lean Frontiers, Inc.

Creating an Effective Management System

Creating an Effective Management System

Integrating Policy Deployment, TWI, and Kata

Patrick Graupp
Skip Steward
Brad Parsons

CRC Press
Taylor & Francis Group
Boca Raton London New York

CRC Press is an imprint of the
Taylor & Francis Group, an **informa** business

A PRODUCTIVITY PRESS BOOK

First edition published in 2020
by Routledge/Productivity Press
52 Vanderbilt Avenue, 11th Floor New York, NY 10017

2 Park Square, Milton Park, Abingdon, Oxon OX14 4RN, UK

© 2020 by Taylor & Francis Group, LLC

Routledge/Productivity Press is an imprint of Taylor & Francis Group, an Informa business

No claim to original U.S. Government works

Printed on acid-free paper

International Standard Book Number-13: 978-1-138-59495-1 (Paperback)

International Standard Book Number-13: 978-1-138-59498-2 (Hardback)

International Standard Book Number-13: 978-0-429-48849-8 (eBook)

Library of Congress Cataloging-in-Publication Data

LoC Data here

**Visit the Taylor & Francis Web site at
http://www.taylorandfrancis.com**

Dedicated to passionate, engaged people at all levels of organizations, and specifically employees at Baptist Memorial Health Care, who courageously practice continuous improvement. You teach and inspire us!

Contents

Contents

About the Authors

Patrick Graupp began his training career at the SANYO Electric Corporate Training Center in Japan after graduating with Highest Honors from Drexel University in 1980. There he learned to deliver TWI from his mentor Kazuhiko Shibuya. Mr. Shibuya was trained by Kenji Ogawa, who was trained by the four TWI Inc. trainers sent from the United States to help Japan rebuild industry in 1951. Patrick earned an MBA from Boston University while leading Sanyo's global training effort. He was later promoted to the head of Human Resources for SANYO North America Corp. in San Diego, CA where he settled.

Patrick partnered with Bob Wrona in 2001 to conduct TWI pilot projects in Syracuse, NY that became the foundation for the TWI Institute that has since trained a rapidly expanding global network of almost 2,000 certified trainers who are now delivering TWI training in the manufacturing, health care, construction, energy, and service industries in the United States and around the globe. He is the author of several books on the TWI methodologies including *The TWI Workbook: Essential Skills for Supervisors*, a Shingo Research and Professional Publication Prize Recipient for 2007 now in its 2nd Edition, *Implementing TWI: Creating and Managing a Skills-Based Culture*, which was published in 2010, *Getting to Standard Work in Health Care: Using TWI to Create a Foundation for Quality Care*, published in 2012, and *Building a Global Learning Organization: Using TWI to Succeed with Strategic Workforce Expansion in the LEGO Group*, published in 2014 and also a Shingo Prize Recipient.

Skip Steward earned an MBA and is experienced in diverse industries including automotive, machining, food, process, service, and healthcare. He is a Shingo examiner, a Certified Quality Engineer (CQE), a Quality Management System Auditor, a certified Six Sigma Black Belt, and a certified Lean Champion. Mr. Steward is a certified trainer in TWI Job Instructions (JI), Job Relations (JR), and Job Methods (JM). He is an award-winning leader who has implemented streamlined business systems that deliver significant contributions to the bottom line, while increasing employee performance and improving productivity. He is recognized for superior project management and communication skills; he has spoken both nationally and internationally.

Mr. Steward currently serves as Vice President and Chief Improvement Officer at Baptist Memorial Health Care headquartered in Memphis, TN where he develops, directs, and implements performance improvement activities identifying inefficiencies; implementing strategies to improve quality, service, and finances; and fostering a culture of continuous improvement and excellence.

Brad Parsons currently serves as the CEO of NEA Baptist Health System. NEA Baptist is an integrated delivery system located in Jonesboro, AR. Brad has served as CEO of NEA Baptist Memorial Hospital since June of 2012; he was named CEO of the medical group in December of 2015.

NEA Baptist is part of Baptist Memorial Health Care, a physician and hospital organization based in Memphis, TN. Brad joined Baptist Memorial Healthcare Corporation in August of 2008 as an Assistant Administrator at Baptist – Golden Triangle, a 350-bed regional medical center in Columbus, MS. In August of 2010, Brad was promoted to CEO and Administrator of Baptist-Union City, in Union City, TN. Prior to joining Baptist, Brad spent five years as an Assistant Vice President at Decatur General Hospital in Decatur, AL.

Brad is originally from Birmingham, AL, where he graduated from Birmingham-Southern College with degrees in Business Administration and Leadership Studies. Brad received two Masters' Degrees from the University of Alabama in Birmingham (UAB) – in Hospital Administration and Business Administration. Brad is a Fellow in the American College of Healthcare Executives and serves on various community and civic boards. He has been married for 15 years to his wife, Carroll Lane, and is the proud father of two daughters and two sons.

Introduction

What Is a Management System?

> Managers fail to diagnose the failures of the fads they adopt; they do not understand them. Most panaceas fail because they are applied antisystemically. They need not be, but to do otherwise requires an understanding of systems and the ability to think systemically.
>
> **Dr. Russell Ackoff**

To understand what a Management System is or might be, first one must understand what a *system* is. At its most basic, a system is *a whole that cannot be divided into independent parts*. The human body, for example, is a system consisting of many interdependent subsystems like the circulatory system, the respiratory system, the digestive system, and so on. Any one of these parts, cannot function and survive on its own. In the interactions of the subsystems, the whole system, the body, lives and thrives. The parts of a system satisfy three conditions[1]:

1. Each of these parts affects the whole and is necessary.
2. None of the parts has an independent effect on the whole. The way that each part affects the whole depends on what the other parts are doing. The parts are interdependent and connected.
3. No subgroup of parts has an independent effect on the whole. If parts of a system are grouped into subgroups or subsystems, they have the same properties as do the individual parts. None has an independent effect.

---

[1] Taken from YouTube videos of Dr. Russell Ackoff and conversations Skip had with Dr. Alan M. Barstow, Director and Senior Scholar of Organizational Dynamics at the University of Pennsylvania.

What we see from these conditions is that the properties that make up a system are the product of the interaction of the system's parts, not the sum of those parts taken separately. In other words, the properties of the whole are derived from the interaction of the parts and not the actions of those individual parts. We cannot know or understand the purpose of the system just by taking apart and analyzing its component parts. The purpose of the system is only revealed when we look at the role of the system in the broader context of what it is trying to accomplish.

How we tend to understand things in life and work usually takes just the opposite course, through analysis and analytical thinking – taking things apart. This leads to knowledge, to figuring out how things work; what we like to call "knowhow." The modern go-to mode for learning and development is to understand the components first and then try to put them together to make sense of the whole. Take management education, for example, where highly motivated and well-intentioned people learn about organizing work. They take classes in finance, human resources, marketing, operations, economics, business ethics, etc., under the assumption that, once a person understands all the separate functions of a business, she will be able to assimilate that knowledge into an understanding of the whole. This is analytical thinking, and most organizations, whether in business, healthcare, education, or government, maintain a structure that is a reflection of this analytical style of thinking. The work of the organization is broken down into parts, specialties, where "experts" in each field contribute to part of the overall system. It is hoped that at the end of the day there will be some capable person who synthesizes these various parts into an understandable, and workable, whole.

Synthesis before Analysis

Dr. Russell Ackoff, a pioneer and leader of systems thinking and management science throughout the second half of the last century, preached "synthesis before analysis." He believed that, counter to what the management world intuitively believes, improving the parts of a system will *not* improve the performance of the whole. In fact, it can even destroy an organization. Likewise, attempting to take a system apart and study the component parts in order to understand the whole will not help us understand the role or purpose of the system itself. For Ackoff, systematic thinking is a prerequisite to understanding purpose because, while analysis can give you knowledge, synthesis will give you wisdom.

A famous thought experiment Ackoff used to demonstrate these system fundamentals with his students at the Wharton School, where he was Professor Emeritus for the last 23 years of his life, was to have them come up with the very *best* automobile by selecting the very *best* components from approximately 500 different car companies. For example, by taking the engine of a Rolls Royce, the transmission of a Mercedes, the suspension of a Ferrari, the steering of a Porsche, the braking of a BMW, the interior of a Cadillac, and so on, the students could theoretically ask engineers to assemble these parts and create the world's *best* car. Would it work? The answer was obviously no because, in the first place, the parts would not fit together. Even if they did, the performance of the car, of the system, would be dependent on how all the parts interacted with each other. Each of these *best* components was designed to work in different car designs and configurations with different performance expectations and varying technical parameters. Therefore, they would not perform optimally together in spite of each part being the *best* in its class.

Yet, organizations routinely run on the assumption that if we could only obtain the *best* CEO, the *best* operations manager, the *best* HR director, the *best* financial wizard, the *best* designers and engineers, all the *best* employees, then, and only then, would we be able to succeed and be the *best* in our business. Moreover, with this analytical mindset, these same organizations endeavor to fix systemic problems by correcting performance in individual parts of the system. In other words, if a problem is encountered and identified in some part of the system the solution must be to "fix" the problem at its source by making performance there the *best* it can be.

The purpose of a car is to carry people from point A to point B, but no individual part of the car will get you from point A to point B. The engine is essential to moving the vehicle, but by itself, with no chassis, drive shaft, axels, wheels, seats, or body, it will just sit on the ground. The utility and value of the automobile derives only from the interaction of all the car's parts. A system, the car in this case, is never the sum of its parts but the product of their interactions. If the parts of the car do not interact well, then we certainly do not have an effective transportation vehicle; working on any one part of that system to improve the performance, without regard to how all the parts interact, will be an exercise in futility. Likewise, when disassembling the system in order to analyze it, looking only at the inherent value of the individual parts, we lose sight of the purpose of the whole enterprise. When we do that, the system, as well as the individual parts, loses its essential properties.

Ackoff continued questioning his students on analyzing a car in order to explain the limitations of analysis on understanding purpose. Would taking apart the car help us to understand why the engine is in the front of the vehicle and not the back? Would disassembling the car and analyzing its parts teach us why the car holds six passengers instead of just two? If we take apart an English car, will this help us to figure out why it has the steering wheel on the right side instead of the left? Explanations to these types of questions will always lie outside of the system. While analysis can provide knowledge of how things work it will never give understanding of why things are the way they are. The behavior of the system can only be understood through synthesis. In management, as well, we can only understand, and affect, the behavior of the management system as a whole by knowing the parts and the way they interact.

A good example in actual management practice is the Emergency Department of any hospital in which a significant percentage of the ED patients need some type of service outside of the ED such as an X-ray, CT scan, or lab work. If the hospital buys the *best* radiology and laboratory equipment and hires the *best* staff in these departments, would that make its ED the *best* Emergency Department? Not necessarily. The overall quality of the ED will depend on the quality of the interactions of these departments and the way the management system deals with the differing challenges and goals of each area. If each department acts on and responds to its own priorities while ignoring the priorities of the others, then patients moving between departments will experience inefficiencies and perhaps dysfunction.

In this sense, what we are really trying to do in any enterprise is to use a social system to manage a physical system. While the technical aspects of any organization may lie in its physical system – the equipment, the methods, the technology, the infrastructure, etc. – analyzing these details will not lead to the organizational performance we seek. The behavior exhibited in the social system will ultimately define how well these physical assets are used. Looking for and finding wisdom and purpose are results of synthesis and how the social system allows the different parts of the organization to interact effectively.

The Gear Train Model[2]

The statistician George Box said, "All models are wrong, but some are useful." Moreover, he elaborated that while "the ability to devise simple but evocative models is the signature of the great scientist," often the mark of mediocrity is to overelaborate and impose strictness and meaning on a model as if it truly, and exactly, represented real-world conditions. When commenting on "useful" models, Box stated,

> For such a model there is no need to ask the questions "Is the model true?" If "truth" is to be the "whole truth" the answer must be "No". The only question of interest is "Is the model illuminating and useful?"[3]

With these cautions in mind, we would like to present a model that describes the Management System that we call the Gear Train Model. In our efforts over the past five years working together to help people in organizations "connect the dots" between various elements of the management system we have collectively helped put into play, we have found that this model not only helps create understanding but also generates enthusiasm from top management all the way down to the front lines. In other words, it meets Box's criteria of being both illuminating and useful. It is a way, however imperfect (as all models are), to *synthesize* the various activities necessary to improve performance throughout the whole system by allowing people to mentally picture how all these activities and initiatives work together.

Simply put, the Gear Train Model is a visual display showing how different elements of a management system interact as interconnected gears that spin together in a "gear train." (See Figure I.1.) The largest gear at the top could represent our strategic planning with goals and objectives for the entire organization. These directives are then handed down to the next level of gears, different departments or value streams in the organization, which create their own set of local activities to align with the broader strategic initiatives. We could call this the tactical planning level. The next level of gears would represent teams working within the departments or value

---

[2] Taken from Brian L. Joiner, *Fourth Generation Management: The New Business Consciousness* (New York, NY: McGraw-Hill, Inc., 1994).

[3] Box, G. E. P. (1979), "Robustness in the strategy of scientific model building," in Launer, R. L.; Wilkinson, G. N., *Robustness in Statistics*, Academic Press, pp. 201–236.

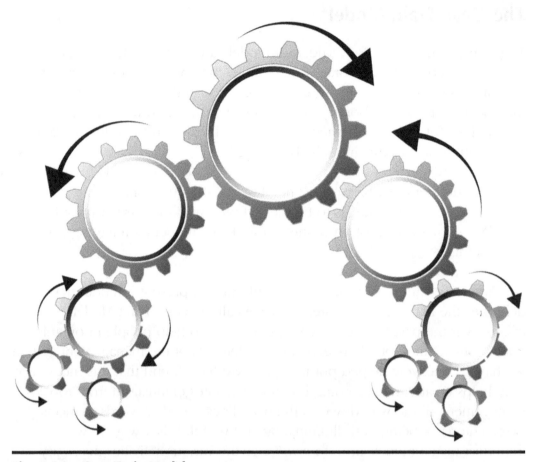

Figure I.1 Gear Train Model

streams on individual projects and challenges that line up with the department plans. A fourth level of gears might represent individual skills applied
by persons assigned to perform functions that bring these local projects to
successful conclusions and help teams achieve their targets and challenges.
(We will get into much more detail on each of these levels in Chapter 2.)

So far, so easy. It is not difficult to comprehend how a complex organization can be viewed, from a management perspective, as a cascading
collection of gears that roll together like a smooth-running machine with one
level of gears driving the next in an efficient and forward system. Nevertheless, it is quite commonplace for people working at the front lines of an
organization not to "get" why they are tasked with working on projects like
a kaizen team or a problem-solving initiative when they are mentally trapped
in a silo that only sees work from their local point of view. They do not see

and are not shown effectively the thinking processes for the different levels of management strategy. "More 'red tape' and corporate bologna," they say. They then complain bitterly that these *distractions* take them away from their *real work* as they wait for the attention paid this "flavor of the month" to fade. They are not thinking, as Ackoff would put it, systematically. The Gear Train Model helps open their minds, through the visualization of different functions in different areas outside their own interacting smoothly as a system, to the larger reality of what the organization is trying to do and how it is trying to do it.

The bigger power of this model, though, and what makes it useful for our purposes in understanding management systems, is in seeing what makes gear trains run smoothly or not. We'll touch on many of these points throughout this book. Interestingly, the principles of gear trains line up quite nicely with what makes a management system hum, or not hum, and create easy-to-recognize metaphors for what it takes to create an effective management system.[4] Let's take a look at some of them.

When the Big Gear Turns a Fraction of a Degree, the Smallest Gears Spin Wildly

In a gear train, the Pitch Line Velocity, for example 4"/1", remains constant. This means that the 1-inch gear must turn four times as fast as the 4-inch gear. It's like running through the airport with a child – the child has to run faster just to keep up. If an executive at the top of an organization asks a seemingly simple question like "What happened?" he may not realize the amount of work he has set in motion at every succeeding level. The next level gear says, "I'll go and find out." The next level frantically continues the search: "What's going on? Why did this happen?" The little gears are now whirling in a frenzy: "I'm looking! I'm looking!"

Not All Gears Are Engaged

Gears in the gear train may be disengaged because we "clutch" them in and out or, perhaps, because their teeth have worn or been damaged. The gear train itself may be in disrepair due to neglect and lack of maintenance. A key

---

[4] We are greatly indebted here to discussions with Charles D. Schultz, an expert on gears and gear systems (beyta.com).

factor here would be the lack of attention to lubrication. In a management system, as well, the problem of "disengaged employees" can be a big one. Just because we have brought people into our organization doesn't mean they are fully engaged in the work and responsibilities we give them, especially when it comes to the motivation and drive it takes toward helping move the organization toward its goals. Most importantly, because each gear is connected in a chain, the negative effects from even a single disengaged person will ripple throughout the entire organization.

Gear Teeth Wear Out or are Damaged When (1) There Is Not Enough Lubrication or (2) They are Bearing Too Much Load

The most important part about the gear train is the part you can't see, the lubrication. Your gear train is probably in trouble when you see "gunk" in the mechanism; early signs of trouble are discoloration of the metal surface, discoloration of the lubricant, noise, vibration, and a funny smell. In our Gear Train Model, we look at lubrication in a management system as representing the human relations within the organization that keep the connections between departments, functions, and individuals running smoothly. When these human relations are neglected or poorly managed, it is not too difficult to detect, in the faces, words, behaviors, and attitude of the people, plenty of "noise, vibration, and a funny smell." When people are "bearing too much load," not only in the amount of work, but more significantly, in the lack of support from the system, the natural result is the gear breaks down.

You Adjust Speed and Load to the Slowest Gear

Gear trains are usually designed to cut down the power of the motor because few processes can run at speeds faster than the power coming in. In other words, motor speed must be reduced to the process speed so that the mechanism doesn't burn itself out. As stated in the previous point, when a gear bears too much load it breaks. Organizations and their leaders risk failure when they attempt to drive their management systems beyond their designed capability. The imperative here, of course, is to improve the system, not just make it work harder. In a gear train, that can be done by changing the size of the gears to match the load, increasing the smoothness of the process (lubrication!), looking at the prime energy source (e.g., electric vs.

diesel), redesigning the size of the gear teeth, using different materials, etc. Whether you work with a mechanical gear train or a human organization, the key is to build capability and flexibility into the system.

Gear Trains Fail When Some External Object or Force Gets Jammed into Them

This is the proverbial monkey wrench thrown into the system; the metaphor is used regularly to describe how human systems are disrupted when an unexpected change is forced onto an unwilling workforce. As noted in the previous point, change can create improvement in a system only when it is effectively designed.

"Locked in Loads" Create Additional Energy over and above that Coming from the Power Source

We might assume that all the power in a gear train emanates from the input motor. But, in actuality, everything in the gear train acts like a spring adding additional "power" to the system. This is caused by the interaction of all the component parts and the stretching of the raw material creating the spring reaction. In human systems, we might call that synergy (the phenomenon of our efforts creating results even greater than the individual inputs). The key to strong leadership is harnessing the inherent power of each group and individual (each gear in the gear train) to move us dynamically toward our goals.

Gear Trains Can Be Added to and Powered by the Main Gear Train

You can add functions to a gear train, and a gear train can run another gear train. A well-designed system can be the source of great energy, output, and innovation but only when it runs smoothly.

Trust the Process

As we see in the Gear Train Model, a critical component to making the whole thing work is the lubrication. In a management system, we can see human relations as this lubrication that binds departments and individuals at every level of the organization. When relations between individuals and departments are strained or broken, optimal performance is not achieved.

It is common in organizations to think of people as working in silos, fully separated and divorced from all the other silos on the cornfield. This is a fitting but limited image. We often hear that more than 90% of the problems we face are more effectively solved somewhere other than where they were found. That means that there is always some connection between silos, despite their standing alone in all their individual and separate glory. We might assume that breaking down these silos would be recommended to make the system work better, but what would that look like? We can allow people to interact more freely with their counterparts in different departments, but the different functions of the organization must still be carried out by people, using their specialty skills and experience, tasked with the specific duties of each area. All the functions contribute in some way to the final product or service being offered. Whether we recognize it or not, *there is a management system* at play in every enterprise; the challenge is to find the system that enables positive and productive interaction between roles.

Another way of looking at the concept of a management system is with a sports analogy. Sports comparisons are revealing because the results of "how they play the game" are seen swiftly and often dramatically. There is a winner and a loser (though sometimes they tie, but that is not the purpose of the competition). Moreover, when we see a team continuously win, it becomes clear that it is doing something unique and special that allows it to remain ahead of perennial rivals.

Nick Saban, coach of the University of Alabama football team, has won five national titles in the last nine years (as of the 2018 season) in addition to winning the national championship as head coach of LSU in 2003.[5] He is recognized for his leadership style by business leaders in numerous books and magazines such as *Fortune* and *Forbes*. He was ranked #12 on *Fortune*'s 2018 list of The World's 50 Greatest Leaders, ahead of Apple's Tim Cook at #14. He is famous for what is called The Process, "a methodical, efficient approach to organizational management,"[6] that allows his teams to dominate over time even though they are composed of different players each year as student players come and go.

For all his wins, in his coaching style Saban does not put emphasis on the final score. In fact, Saban is often seen angrily chewing out a player for

---

[5] Full disclosure: Brad and Skip are rabid fans of the Crimson Tide and Nick Saban.
[6] *Fortune Magazine*, How Nick Saban Keeps Alabama Football Rolling, April 23, 2018.

having failed an assignment even when the scoreboard reads 55–0 in their favor. It is easy to mistake Saban as the coach of the losing team when he is seen scowling at small things that his team is not executing properly. The "win" for Saban is not the final score but "how we played the game," where he can find seemingly small items to continue to harp on even when the score is largely in his favor. What he insists on, from both his assistant coaches and his players, is to "focus on the process." The natural result of that focus will be wins and championships.

From Saban's point of view, there are many variables out of any coach's or players' control, and the only thing that can be controlled is how each individual player performs his role for the team, otherwise referred to as The Process. Early in his career when he was head coach at Michigan State University, Saban worked with psychiatry professor Lionel Rose, and together they broke down football games, even entire seasons, into smaller, more manageable pieces that could be practiced. What they found is that excellence is a matter of steps – excel at the first thing, then the next, then the next. Games are won at the fringes, and the team that performs more small things right will prevail in the end. The Process is about focusing on what must be done in each play, any one of which only lasts seven seconds, and overcoming the obstacles that are in front of you right in the moment without getting distracted by the myriad of things that might happen.

The lesson for us is that there is a system that, when followed with discipline and resolve, can be applied and sustained over time to create more victories than losses. Each member of the team executing each play has a specific role and function that must be practiced and then followed precisely in order for the whole team, the whole system, to function cohesively in order to win the play and, eventually, the game. In practices and workouts as well, he makes sure that each drill is run perfectly and the team is able to execute as a whole. Interestingly, the components of The Process include what players do both on and off the field, academically and personally as well as athletically. This process includes preparing young men mentally and physically for football but also for becoming college graduates, developing skills for life outside of football.

When we talk about organizations getting their people out of their silos, what must be focused on is how these people "play the game" *after* we free them up to interact with other functions within the system. They are not acting alone just as any one "superstar" player will not be able to win the game single handedly. Maybe the team will get lucky one day and the "superstar" player will "save the day" with a "miraculous play" that only a true superstar could perform. But to win consistently, over time, all members of the squad must be consistently executing their roles to perfection as a team. Learning how to do that will be the theme of this book.

Conclusion

Let's remember, "All models are wrong, but some are useful." It may be helpful to think about our people as living in silos, divorced and separated from all their counterparts working busily in their own silos. But the reality is that an enterprise works as a system and each "cog in the wheel" is there to serve a purpose. If any one function served no purpose in our organization it would have been eliminated years ago in the relentless pursuit of cutting costs in business practice. Therefore, the focus must be on the process and the way all those gears work together as system.

The purpose of this book is *not* to attempt to define what makes a model management system – what specific programs or methodologies we think you should put into to play in your organization. Rather, what we want to do is outline key elements that must be in place, and how they work together as a "system," to achieve overall success in the enterprise. Every business culture is unique unto itself and must discover and develop its own chemistry that fits its purpose. We encourage you to always reflect on your own management system as you read this book and how its components connect, or do not connect. How could you do that better compared to what you're doing right now?

Successful organizations incorporate basic principles into their daily management that are universal and timeless, principles that speak to and guide the selection of programs and methodologies that can lead the organization to success. We will try to lay out what these principles might be, as well as the functional elements of a management system that turns them into daily activity. These fundamentals are no secret; indeed, they have been working for millennia, but being able to put them together in a well-functioning system takes skill and dedication.

The authors have been working together for the past five years on enhancing and developing the management system of a large multi-hospital healthcare system in the mid-South, though they also have deep experience working in the manufacturing and service sectors. Their experiences form the core content of this book. And while you may not work in healthcare yourself, most people will have enough personal experience with the healthcare system to understand our examples. Whether your management system is in manufacturing, service, government, the arts, or healthcare, the principles upon which success is founded are the same. While we will try to explain our thinking and concepts by giving examples of programs and methodologies we have used, like TWI and Kata, we do not suggest that you necessarily use these programs. Patrick's TWI mentor, Mr. Kazuhiko Shibuya, told him a long time ago when he was a young TWI trainer, "It doesn't really matter what program you use, so long as you apply it diligently." We believe that you will succeed in whatever program or methodology you decide to use, as long as you apply it diligently following basic principles.

What is of paramount importance, though, is that you understand how the programs and methodologies you choose to put into play are governed by the management system. Developing a strong management system can be done by following principles of how people and organization function. If you don't construct your management system well, it will form on its own outside of your control.

Defining Organizational Purpose

1

Chapter 1

How Systems Function Smoothly

Let's start our discussion of management systems by asking the question, "What elements should we put into play in the system?" If a system, by definition, is "a set of connecting things or parts forming a complex whole," then putting the correct pieces in the correct places should be a unique challenge, and no two successful management systems would, or should, have the same combination of components. Finding just the right "recipe" for success is what every enterprise seeks. How we think about this puzzle is critical – do we assume there is one correct answer and undertake a fruitless search for that panacea, or do we recognize that we don't know the answer, because no one ever does, and that we must learn as we go along?

One of the earliest criticisms Toyota managers from Japan had when they saw the American deployment of the vaunted Toyota Production System (TPS), what is more generally called Lean, was that Americans focused solely on "tools" while ignoring the most important part of TPS, the people and their culture. Art Smalley, an expert on TPS who worked and learned at Toyota in Japan, tells the story of an early group of American disciples who, after studying a *kamishibai* style production control system using color coded cards at a Japanese Toyota plant, went to great lengths to replicate the same system in their home plant in the United States. When they returned to Japan the following year for a follow-up tour, they were surprised to see that the system they had struggled so diligently to implement at home was no longer in use at the Japanese plant. "We've moved on to something else," the Toyota workers explained. What the frustrated Americans failed to understand was that the tools, in and of themselves, were not the important thing. They were not the "secret" to how to successfully run a plant. What they missed was the culture of continuous refinement of the process, a culture that is a moving target, always evolving.

Over the last five years, Skip and Brad have been instrumental in applying Lean style thinking and practice to a hospital system in the mid-South; when another large and famous hospital's Lean experts were touring one of their facilities, Skip was asked, "Where is your Value Stream Map?" Skip replied that they did not have a Value Stream Map, to which one of the experts, incredulously, countered, "How can you have a Lean system without a Value Stream Map?" Skip told him that in his facilities, where they didn't really use the word "Lean," that they were experimenting with different pieces in their management system that made sense and worked well together. The Value Stream Map was not one of them in that department at that time.

Every organization is unique, and there is no "success formula." We can experiment our way forward finding components that work effectively within the context of our own history, culture, style, and circumstances: Amazon only hires people who are highly skilled in their specialties, while Toyota looks mainly for people who have a work attitude that matches the culture and then teaches them the skills they will need to do their jobs. The two companies have different management systems, and both are successful at how they manage. What is more, that formula is always changing. What worked last year, the *kamishibai* card system of random audits and checks, for example, will not always be the best tool as our management system evolves and discovers or develops new means of accomplishing the same goals.

However, while the structural patterns of successful organizations may differ and change over time, there exist common guidelines on how management systems function smoothly and effectively. In our Gear Train Model, which we looked at in the Introduction, we saw how certain principles of gear trains (e.g., proper lubrication) always apply, no matter what the machine is designed to do on whatever scale. In human systems as well, certain principles guide the success of the overall system and must be followed.

Based on Principles

Stephen Covey, author of *The Seven Habits of Highly Effective People* and *Principled Centered Leadership*, told us, "There are three constants in life … change, choice and principles." As human beings, we have the freedom to *choose* how we react and adapt to the *change* that is constantly taking place around us, but the key to our success will be based on whether our choices are guided by *principles*. Covey explained that principles are like lighthouses, we don't break them, we break ourselves against them. On the other hand, when we use them well, they help us to steer safely around the rocky coastlines of life. And, like the Law of Gravity, they are always true. When we attempt to defy the Law of Gravity, it does not end well.

The following principle is, we feel, relatable and instructive for all: *Mutual relationships only survive when there is mutual benefit.* Let's look at what makes this a "law of (human) nature." How many of us have a relationship, be it personal or professional, in which we feel we are giving everything and getting nothing, or not nearly enough, in return? How long will that relationship continue? Even if the relationship is necessary ("I need this job!"), there will always be negative repercussions, usually in the form of attitude and behavior, from the person who feels wronged. In a family, in a business, in a community, or in a friendship, whenever we depend on mutual relationships to fulfill our life expectations, we must consider the needs of others in addition to our own. When we go against this principle, we go down a path of disappointment and failure. That's what makes it a guiding principle of life.

We must follow specific principles when making the selection of elements for a management system. If your principle, your guiding "truth," is "People are lazy and must be forced to work" (aka: Theory X), then your management system will reflect some sort of authoritarian command-and-control structure with its associated tools and programs. If your principle is "People are responsible and want to do a good job" (aka: Theory Y), then your management system should, if you really want to live this principle, reflect a more engaging and participative style of leadership. Your management system, and what pieces you put into play in your management system, will embody the principles by which your organization lives.

Successful companies strive to live by principles that guide the daily actions taken within their management systems. For example, Amazon defines their Leadership Principles[1] as:

■ Customer Obsession
■ Ownership

---

[1] Company website: www.amazon.jobs/en/principles.

- Invent and Simplify
- Are Right, A Lot
- Learn and Be Curious
- Hire and Develop the Best
- Insist on the Highest Standards
- Think Big
- Bias for Action
- Frugality
- Earn Trust
- Dive Deep
- Have Backbone; Disagree and Commit
- Deliver Results

These principles "are integral to virtually everything that we do at Amazon," according to an Amazon manager, and "they have served as a constant that everyone can use to calibrate and measure against." This has been especially critical, he explained, as the company has grown with rapid speed over the past five to six years. Once the organization grows beyond the "line of sight" of leaders at the executive and director level, even at the senior manager level, it depends on these core principles to keep everything moving in the right direction. What is more, Amazon uses its Leadership Principles as a basis for assessing new-hire candidates as well as a key component of its performance assessment and rigorous promotion process.

This book will focus on how principles are applied in the management system to ensure that it is working in alignment with the laws of nature, like the Law of Gravity. In other words, the book will look at how we design and operate a management system, starting with putting the right pieces in place, so that it follows the principles we follow. If we had long and in-depth experience working at Amazon, we could write a book on how to create a strong management system following the Amazon principles shown above. But our book must be based on what we believe in and follow. So, first, we must state our beliefs, best reflected by the *10 Shingo Guiding Principles*[2]:

- Respect Every Individual
- Lead with Humility
- Seek Perfection

---

[2] Gerhard Plenert, *Discovery Excellence: An Overview of the Shingo Model and Its Guiding Principles* (Boca Raton, FL: CRC Press, 2018).

- Embrace Scientific Thinking
- Focus on Process
- Assure Quality at the Source
- Flow & Pull Value
- Think Systemically
- *Create Constancy of Purpose*
- Create Value for the Customer

The Shingo Institute, famous for its Shingo Prize for Operational Excellence, which began in 1988, was named after Dr. Shigeo Shingo, who worked extensively as a consultant with Taiichi Ono and documented the processes and philosophy of the Toyota Management System. More recently, since 2008, the institute began focusing its attention on assessing organizational culture as a whole, not just tools and programs, "including all the interactions between the various functions of the organization."[3] They were searching for the answer to the big question, "How does one sustain excellence?" In the process of coming up with this expanded model, from which they arrived at the 10 principles, they fell upon three insights that directly tie principle-based behavior to the management system[4]:

Insight #1: Ideal Results Require Ideal Behavior
Insight #2: Purpose and Systems Drive Behavior
Insight #3: Principles Inform Ideal Behavior

Putting these insights together, we can see how, as leaders of our organization, we must create *systems* that drive the *ideal, principle-based behavior* that generates the *ideal results* we need to realize our *purpose*. One of our authors, Skip, is a Shingo Examiner. He and his fellow examiners, when they are called upon to do site assessments, look to see whether the target company's management systems are in alignment with these 10 principles and whether their management systems are representative of the principles or working against them. When they are aligned with the principles, it is more likely that the management system will deliver on its promise. The pieces we put into play in our management system matter; how they align and interact with each other will determine whether our system works successfully, just like in a well-tuned gear train.

---

[3] Ibid.
[4] Ibid.

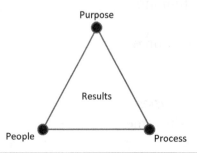

Figure 1.1   Three Dimensions of the Management System

You may notice that, of the 10 principles, the first two are focused on *people*, the next five are connected to *process*, and the next two to *purpose*. The final principle, Create Value for the Customer, is related to *results*. The three dimensions of Purpose – People – Process sum up the critical areas that need to be captured in the management system with the final dimension, Results, being the outcome of the former three (see Figure 1.1). This book is organized around this model. Part 1 will focus on *Purpose*, Part 2 on *People*, and Part 3 on *Process*. The final chapter will sum up how these three parts give us the *Results* we need to sustain the organization over the long term.

Management System Defined

What is a management system? We've been discussing it for some pages now as if it were an assumption not needing any explanation. There are many concepts and theories on how to manage, everything from Peter Drucker's *Management by Objective* to Peter Senge's *Learning Organization* to Taiichi Ono's *Toyota Production System* to *Six Sigma* to *Lean*. As we intimated at the outset, there is no right or wrong, or good or bad, to any one style of management; in the end, we learn something from all of them and put together elements in what becomes our own organization's unique management system. Every enterprise, whether the people inside know it or not, has a management system. This management system may have been intentionally conceived and deployed or it could have developed ad hoc. For better or for worse, there is a system, and even if many of its components are really good, they will fail if not integrated properly in the overall management system.

The Toyota production system, however, is not just a production system. I am confident it will reveal its strength as a management system adapted to today's era of global markets and high-level computerized information systems.

Taiichi Ono
June 1987

Many people have thought of Lean as a management system embodied in the "Lean House" model where the two pillars of Just-in-Time and *Jidoka*[5] stand on a foundation of *Heijunka*,[6] Standardized Work, and Kaizen and hold up the roof that represents our results of Quality, Cost, Delivery, and Safety (see Figure 1.2). As Art Smalley puts it, "TPS can be viewed as

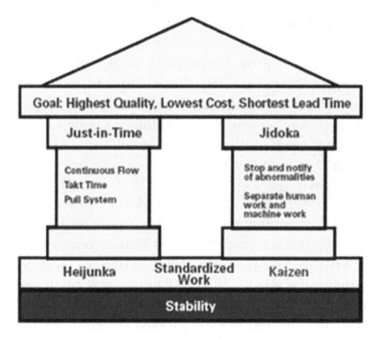

Toyota Production System "House."

Figure 1.2   Lean House Model (Lean.org)

---

[5] *Jidoka* highlights the causes of problems because work stops immediately when a problem first occurs. This leads to improvements in the processes that build in quality by eliminating the root causes of defects (From Lean.org).

[6] *Heijunka* means sequencing or smoothing production. It is defined as "the distribution of production volume and mix evenly over time" (From Leanlab.name).

a 'house' of multiple, interconnected subsystems."[7] Practitioners have believed that if they could master and apply all of the tools and methodologies of the Lean model (Process Flow Mapping, Kanban, 5S, TPM, A3 Problem Solving, Pull Systems, Takt Time, etc.), they would wind up where Toyota is today, a truly Lean enterprise. However, as we saw with the plant that tried to copy Toyota's tools, more is needed. Without understanding the thinking behind the "house," just copying and pasting does not work out in most cases. Simply implementing the tools does not lead to the holy grail of Lean. The tools certainly do work, when applied correctly and diligently, but the results very rarely are sustained and the promised transformation in culture hardly ever takes place without understanding the principles behind Lean.

David Mann picked up the trail here in his groundbreaking 2005 work, *Creating a Lean Culture: Tools to Sustain Lean Conversions*. In it, Mann defined the Lean Management System as something distinct from the Lean Production System: the management system worked to "sustain the gains from implementing Lean production."[8] He characterized the work of Lean, all those tools and methodologies we find in the Lean House, as comprising only 20% of a Lean implementation, while "the remaining 80 percent of the required time and effort is made up of tasks that are less obvious and much more demanding."[9] This larger portion of the work, the management system, consisted of the things needed to sustain the effort over the long term and to change the culture, its habits, and its ways of thinking. As Mann put it, "A company's culture is a *result* of its management system."

More specifically, Mann's work went into detail laying out the implementation of what he saw as the three essential components to a Lean management system: (1) Leader Standard Work, (2) Visual Controls, and (3) Daily Accountability Process. The Lean Production System is, by definition, "lean" with little "waste" in the process that we can fall back on to make up for failures or inconsistencies when discipline in the system wanes. Large inventories of spare parts and work-in-process are examples of this kind of waste. In order to maintain the needed discipline, these three essential components make up a "parallel Lean implementation effort,"[10] with its

[7] Art Smalley, *Four Types of Problems: From Reactive Troubleshooting to Creative Innovation* (Cambridge, MA: Lean Enterprise Institute, 2018).
[8] David Mann, *Creating a Lean Culture: Tools to Sustain Lean Conversions, Third Edition* (Boca Raton, FL: CRC Press, 2015).
[9] Ibid.
[10] Ibid.

careful and continuous eye on how the production is proceeding throughout each hour of each day, and keep the process humming through timely interaction against any deviations that might occur. Speaking of discipline, Mann added a fourth element to the management system, *discipline.* He characterized *discipline* as the fuel that keeps the management system running and in place.

These elements are critical, and we highly recommend studying, internalizing, and practicing Mann's model. As you will see, the three elements, along with discipline, will be called upon throughout the activities we promote in this book. Now that we have a working definition of what a "management system" is, from a Lean perspective at least, we want to take a "deeper dive" into how to make this management system work.

Meta-Processes

We started out this chapter asking the question of what to put into a management system. While the easy answer is, "Whatever works for you," we saw that Mann offered three critical elements that are needed to manage, and maintain, all the other tools, methodologies, programs, skills, and activities we put into play to run our business. This would be a good place to start thinking about your management system. We do not want to tell you how to run your business and what components you should put into your management system. We are not qualified to do so; only you, who are closest to the work and can understand the daily workings of your business and its unique culture, can decide that. However, what we, and several contemplative thought leaders, are discovering is the usefulness of what we like to call meta-processes.

"Meta" is a prefix that means "change," "after," "along with," "among," or "beyond." More specifically, it is a prefix "added to a subject ... that analyzes (itself) at a more abstract, higher level."[11] So the word *metaphysics* refers to the branch of philosophy that goes beyond what can be known simply from physics, like the relationship between mind and matter. A *metamorphosis* is when a complete change in form takes place, like when a caterpillar becomes a butterfly. A *metaconversation* is a conversation about another conversation that has already taken place and *metacriticism* is criticism of

---

[11] Dictionary.com.

another criticism. So, a meta-process would be a process about, and working on, other processes, but from a broader level.

What this means more practically is that meta-processes are programs that, because they look at the work from this broader level, can be applied to any situation and are independent from the details of the work. In other words, they are higher-level patterns that can be used regularly, regardless of the task, problem, or project at hand, that become the modes of behavior and patterns of thinking that constitute the culture of an organization. Mark Rosenthal, a long time Lean thought leader, talks of "meta-patterns" that are "structures that foster deliberate learning; and structures that cause people to actually talk to each other and build working relationships."[12] He says "while the visible structural patterns (of organizations) may be different, the *purpose* of those structural patterns reveals a common way of thinking, or meta-patterns, that are implemented by the various structures we can directly observe."[13]

What are these meta-processes? They are methodologies that "work on the work" and guide both the management of the work and the work practices themselves in ways that build and transform them. As it turns out, they are nothing new. We have long had and deployed these higher levels of thinking, even though we did not call them meta-processes. They serve us well when we purposefully apply them in our management system and use them to build our organization's culture, preferably one based on true principles.

In this book, we will look at three programs we consider meta-processes that we use to create strong management systems in the work we do: Policy Deployment (*Hoshin Kanri*), Kata, and Training Within Industry (TWI). As we've said, each organization must select the components to put into its own unique management systems; we do not want to suggest, in spite of our enthusiasm for them, that these three necessarily be used by you and your organization. We have deep experience with them, and know them well, so we will review them as examples when describing how we think a good management system can and should be built. Here is a (very) quick introduction to each.

---

[12] From conversation with Mark Rosenthal.

[13] Mark Rosenthal, "The Meta-Patterns of Innovation," *Lean Frontiers* (2018). www.leanfrontiers.com/the-meta-patterns-of-innovation/.

Policy Deployment (Hoshin Kanri)

The concepts and practice of Policy Deployment, what the Japanese call *Hoshin Kanri*, are well documented in the literature; it is not our intention to reteach it, nor Kata or TWI for that matter. We have found that the Policy Deployment approach to comprehensively laying out top-level strategic initiatives and then guiding and coaching the implementation system, layer by layer, to each level of the organization is a vital part of creating and maintaining an effective management system. By setting a clear direction for the organization, this practice can *Create Constancy of Purpose*, one of the 10 principles we strive to follow. Pascal Dennis, a Lean expert who focuses on strategic planning and execution, likes to call *Hoshin Kanri* "the nervous system of Lean production" because it addresses, through short-term (one year) and long-term (three to five year) planning, how to identify critical business needs while, most importantly, developing the capability of our people to achieve critical results at all levels in addressing these needs.[14]

What makes Policy Deployment so critical to an effective management system is its ability to create alignment between what is promoted at the highest levels of the organization and what is done on the front lines of the business. This goes to the core of what a management system is trying to do and should not be taken for granted. Dennis describes the challenge this way:

> The leader has to be at home at the level of experience as well as the level of thought. Action without theory is aimless; theory without action is lifeless. Effective leaders move fluidly up and down a ladder of abstraction, between lower-level facts and higher-level concepts. If you speak at high levels of abstraction without having reasoned your way to them from lower levels, what you say is unlikely to be founded in fact. Similarly, if you're mired in lower-level data unable to extract the meaning, what you say is unlikely to motivate team members.[15]

In our experience, Policy Deployment is the anchor of a management system because it holds the ship in a predetermined position and keeps it from drifting. It is a central way to deploy and align strategy in a complex

---

[14] Pascal Dennis, *Lean Production Simplified: A Plain-Language Guide to the World's Most Powerful Production System*, Third Edition (Boca Raton, FL: CRC Press, 2016).

[15] Pascal Dennis, *Getting the Right Things Done: A Leader's Guide to Planning and Execution* (Cambridge, MA: The Lean Enterprise Institute, 2006).

organization as it directs and helps align work that is critically important to achieving organizational goals. It provides the physical place in which employees know they can connect their work to the strategy of the organization (more on this in the next chapter).

Policy Deployment certainly meets our definition of a meta-process because it operates independent of the details of the work at hand. This is a higher level of activity than, say, the *kamishibai* card control system we noted earlier that was used at one time in a Toyota plant as a means of achieving a specific *hoshin* goal. When that goal was accomplished, or when a better way of reaching the goal was found, the process changed. It was dependent on the task at hand. While the tools may change, the management system, with this critical element of Policy Deployment, continues to function and guide the organization.

Kata

Between 2004 and 2009, Mike Rother and his colleagues studied Toyota with the intention of finding "the unseen managerial routines and thinking that lie behind Toyota's success with continuous improvement and adaption."[16] More than just that, they sought to find a way to show how other organizations could develop routines and thinking that would replicate Toyota's success. They called their findings *Toyota Kata.*[17]

The Japanese word *kata* means *pattern* or *form* and can be combined with almost any verb to mean "the way to … " as in "the way to eat sushi" or "the way to hit a baseball." Every Toyota manager Rother and his colleagues observed had a unique leadership style. There were no formal or pre-structured methods of coaching, but over time a pattern emerged as to how managers worked with people. This way of thinking and behaving was so deeply embedded in the culture that the Toyota managers had difficulty explaining their routines or articulating their methods, but there was a method. As Rother explains it, "We came to see that Toyota's management approach involves teaching all organization members a scientific approach and mindset that can be applied to an infinite number of challenges and objectives." This clearly is what we could call a meta-process.

---

[16] Mike Rother, *The Toyota Kata Practice Guide* (New York, NY: McGraw-Hill Education, 2018).

[17] Though it is called Toyota Kata, Patrick spent the first 20 years of his career working for Sanyo Electric, 10 of those years in Japan; he can confirm that the same cultural patterns described by Rother in his work also apply to other Japanese companies.

To illustrate what managerial routines and modes of thinking are used at Toyota, Rother laid out what he called the Improvement Kata with a 4-step process:

STEP 1: Understand the Direction or Challenge
STEP 2: Grasp the Current Condition
STEP 3: Establish the Next Target Condition
STEP 4: Experiment Toward the Target Condition

It is portrayed pictorially in Figure 1.3. Rother found that Toyota managers were willing to let their people "experiment" their way forward to their target conditions, navigating through the uncharted territory of obstacles. In other words, they made it OK for people to fail and to learn from their failures. This is radically different from the typical western style of management in which failure "is not an option" and people regularly fear the ramifications of failure. It fit much more squarely within the scientific method of setting and testing hypotheses for solving problems, the PDCA (Plan – Do – Check – Act) cycle introduced to Japan by Dr. Edward Deming from the United States.[18]

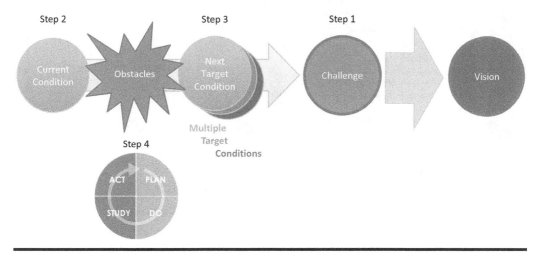

Figure 1.3　Improvement Kata Model

---

[18] "PDCA is oftentimes referred to today as PDSA (Plan - Do - Study - Act)." The irony here is that the Japanese were showing Rother's group, the Americans, how to do things they originally learned from the Americans after the WWII.

With this insight, Rother moved on to answering the question of how organizations outside of Toyota could develop similar routines and ways of thinking by introducing the Coaching Kata. This entailed a series of questions a coach would ask a learner, on a regular coaching cycle, around the Improvement Kata being performed by the learner (see Figure 1.4). In order to develop this culture of coaching employees in the scientific-thinking method, something already well ingrained in Toyota practice, organizations would need a pattern they could practice in order to develop the skill and make it a habit, not unlike a piano student practicing scales or a new golfer practicing his or her swing. These questions, and the discipline around the coaching sessions, provide that pattern. We'll see more in detail in Chapter 6.

As Kata practitioners, we have seen tremendous progress and enthusiasm in organizations in which the Kata thinking pattern has been introduced. It is refreshing and, quite honestly, truly incredible to see employees who were, at best, lukewarm when it came to engaging in traditional Lean activity, become enthusiastic participants in the Kata routines. We believe this is because of the exciting challenge the activity presents to those who are

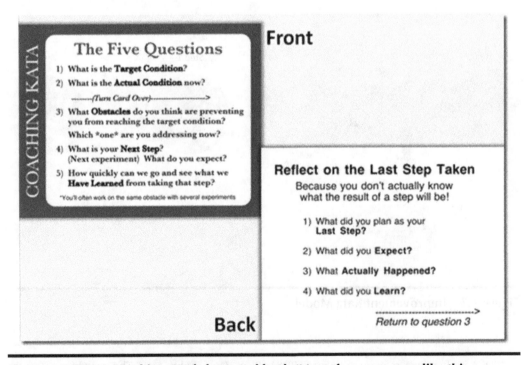

Figure 1.4 Kata Coaching Card, front and back (Many free resources like this are available on the Toyota Kata website)

searching for deeper meaning in their work. People are able to discover, on their own, something new that has the opportunity to make life richer and more fulfilling. As Rother puts it, "The Improvement Kata pattern begins with a sense of direction. It's about striving for a desired new condition with a compass, not a map."[19]

We think the Kata pattern of practice should be ingrained in all decisions; people should experiment with a hypothesis, not fully knowing what the outcome will be. This is a much truer approach to achieving strategic objectives at all levels of an organization.

TWI

Training Within Industry (TWI) is a series of methodologies around core skills needed by front-line supervisors to effectively lead a work force. The supervisor, defined in TWI as "anyone in charge of people or who directs the work of others," is the first point of contact the organization has with each employee. The guidance and direction each employee receives from his or her "supervisor," the person who *supervises* the work, is without doubt the most influential factor in the success of that person's job and the organization overall.

The original three TWI programs, developed during WWII, were based on the Five Needs Model (see Figure 1.5) that originated in the early years of the

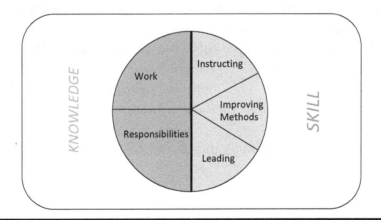

Figure 1.5 Five Needs Model

[19] Mike Rother, *The Toyota Kata Practice Guide* (New York, NY: McGraw-Hill Education, 2018).

Industrial Revolution when management leaders were struggling with the question of what it would take to succeed as a front-line supervisor. They identified two types of knowledge (knowledge of the work and knowledge of responsibilities) and three types of skill (skill in instructing, leading, and improving methods). While the supervisor's knowledge of work and responsibilities was unique to a specific business and organization and would have to be learned locally, the skills were universal. The TWI founders, responding to the wartime need for production, created three training programs that covered these essential skills: Job Instruction, Job Relations, and Job Methods.

SHORT HISTORY OF TWI

The Training Within Industry (TWI) program originated in the United States in the 1940s and was developed out of the need to rapidly train unskilled workers entering the war production workforce as skilled laborers went off to war. The TWI Service was one of the first emergency services established during World War II by the U.S. Government War Production Board; it drafted a national network of professionals from industry to develop techniques to quickly ramp up the production of war materiel.

With the mission to "get out more materials than have ever been thought possible, and at constantly accelerating speed," the TWI Service knew that "the real job had to be done by industry, within industry." The service created supervisory training programs to develop front-line leadership skills, and by the end of the war more than 1.6 million workers in roughly 16,500 plants had received certified training in TWI. The methods were introduced and used in hospitals as well to replace medical professionals who also went off to the war.

Of the 600 client companies monitored by the TWI Service throughout the war:

- 86% increased production by at least 25%,
- 100% reduced training time by 25% or more,
- 88% reduced labor hours by over 25%,
- 55% reduced scrap by at least 25%, and
- 100% reduced grievances by more than 25%.

During the prosperity of post-war America, the TWI program was abandoned and ultimately forgotten. After the war, though, it was introduced to countries around the globe, most significantly Japan, where widespread use of TWI was instrumental in helping create the post-war resurgence of the Japanese economy.

Each program was defined by a 4-Step Method that could be quickly learned and perfected through repetition and practice. Practice and mastery of a fixed pattern, something we just saw with the Kata development, was the way to create regular habits that, in turn, became part of the organization's culture. To stress the practicality and straightforward simplicity of this approach, each method was captured on a pocket-sized card that could be carried at all times and be available when needed.

Job Instruction (JI), the first and still today most widely used of the TWI modules, trains supervisors to "get *a* person to quickly remember to do *a* job correctly, safely and conscientiously." By way of skillfully breaking down a job, using as few, simple words as possible, into the categories of *what* you do, *how* you do it, and *why* you do it that way, the method allows trainers to take learners through repeated cycles of the job, each time layering on these categories and quickly building skill and retention. As long as it is a repeatable process, whether physical, verbal, or mental, the method can be applied to any job, making it versatile in all industries. Figure 1.6 shows the front and back sides of the Job Instruction pocket card. Within the management system, we feel the proper application of JI, for applicable jobs, is irreplaceable in creating ideal standardized behavior for critical processes.

In all industries, there is a pattern of promoting people because they are good workers, not necessarily because they have strong leadership skills. The *Job Relations (JR)* module of TWI focuses on building leadership skill so supervisors are able to bring out the dedication and cooperation of their people, getting the output and quality needed for success. Significantly, the JR approach is humanistic, clearly defining people as unique individuals with opinions, feelings, and motivations that make us different from machines. This may seem to go without saying, but the true soft underbelly of all organizations is the ability to effectively deal with people-related problems and to manage the environment in a way that prevents those problems from occurring and growing. There are clearly right and wrong ways to deal with people. As we will explore more in Part 2 of this book, the JR foundations and problem-solving method (see Figure 1.7) directly apply to the principles of *Respect Every*

JOB INSTRUCTION

HOW TO GET READY TO INSTRUCT

Before instructing people on how to do a job:

1. **MAKE A TIMETABLE FOR TRAINING**

   Who to train …
       For which work …
           By what date …

2. **BREAK DOWN THE JOB**

   List **Important Steps**
   Select **Key Points**
   Safety factors are always Key Points

3. **GET EVERYTHING READY**

   The proper equipment, tools, materials,
   and whatever is needed to aid instruction

4. **ARRANGE THE WORKSITE**

   Neatly, as in actual working conditions

HOW TO INSTRUCT

Step 1 – PREPARE THE WORKER
- Put the person at ease
- State the job
- Find out what the person already knows
- Get the person interested in learning the job
- Place the person in the correct position

Step 2 – PRESENT THE OPERATION
- Tell, show, and illustrate one **Important Step** at a time
- Do it again stressing **Key Points**
- Do it again stating **reasons for Key Points**
Instruct clearly, completely, and patiently, but don't give more information than can be mastered at one time.

Step 3 – TRY-OUT PERFORMANCE
- Have the person do the job—correct errors
- Have the person explain each **Important Step** to you as they do the job again
- Have the person explain each **Key Point** to you as they do the job again
- Have the person explain **reasons for Key Points** to you as they do the job again
Make sure the person understands
*Continue until **you** know **they** know.*

Step 4 – FOLLOW UP
- Put the person on their own.
- Designate who the person goes to for help
- Check on the person frequently
- Encourage questions
- Taper off extra coaching and close follow-up

**IF THE WORKER HASN'T LEARNED,
THE INSTRUCTOR HASN'T TAUGHT**

Figure 1.6   Job Instruction Card, front and back

Individual and *Lead with Humility*. We have seen this become a huge connection point for employee engagement in the overall work of the organization.

The *Job Methods (JM)* module of TWI is "a practical plan to help you produce *greater quantities* of *quality products* in *less time* by making the best use of the Manpower, Machines and Materials now available." In the same way, JM in healthcare "will help you deliver *higher quality patient care more efficiently* by making the best use of the people, equipment, and supplies now available." The key is that we make *best use* of the resources *now available* to us in doing the work. The JM method was the inspiration for the kaizen movement in Japan in the early 1950s. At its heart, JM is a means of "questioning with a purpose" in order to find ideas for improvement from the many details of the job. With a structured method of looking for opportunities to Eliminate, Combine, Rearrange, or Simplify those details, we can

JOB RELATIONS

A SUPERVISOR GETS RESULTS THROUGH PEOPLE

FOUNDATIONS FOR GOOD RELATIONS

Let Each Worker Know How He/She Is Doing
Figure out what you expect of the person
Point out ways to improve

Give Credit When Due
Look for extra or unusual performance
Tell the person while it's "hot"

Tell People in Advance About Changes That Will Affect Them
Tell them why if possible
Work with them to accept the change

Make Best Use of Each Person's Ability
Look for abilities not now being used
Never stand in a person's way

PEOPLE MUST BE TREATED AS INDIVIDUALS

HOW TO HANDLE A PROBLEM

DETERMINE OBJECTIVE

STEP 1 – GET THE FACTS
- Review the record
- Find out what rules and customs apply
- Talk with individuals concerned
- Get opinions and feelings
Be sure you have the whole story

STEP 2 – WEIGH AND DECIDE
- Fit the facts together
- Consider their bearings on each other
- What possible actions are there?
- Check practices and policies
- Consider objective and effect on individual, group, and production
Don't jump to conclusions

STEP 3 – TAKE ACTION
- Are you going to handle this yourself?
- Do you need help in handling?
- Should you refer this to your supervisor?
- Watch the timing of your action
Don't pass the buck

STEP 4 – CHECK RESULTS
- How soon will you follow up?
- How often will you need to check?
- Watch for changes in output, attitudes, and relationships
Did your action help production?

DID YOU ACCOMPLISH YOUR OBJECTIVE?

Figure 1.7   Job Relations Card, front and back

find a better way to do almost any job we set out to improve. The four steps of JM are shown in Figure 1.8.

We have seen JM serve as an idea generator, or an idea activator, and as a vehicle to improve all processes, even those that are perceived by our people as working fairly well. People intuitively know there is waste in their work, but JM systematically identifies that waste and helps eliminate it, creating more efficient and sustainable processes. Significantly, we have seen JM create the "a-ha" moments for teams and leaders when use of this improvement skill allows them to see the power of a connected management system. In other words, having a real taste of your ability to make your own job better puts everything else in perspective and you understand, maybe for the first time, the real purpose of the management system and all its components in driving the organization toward the future.

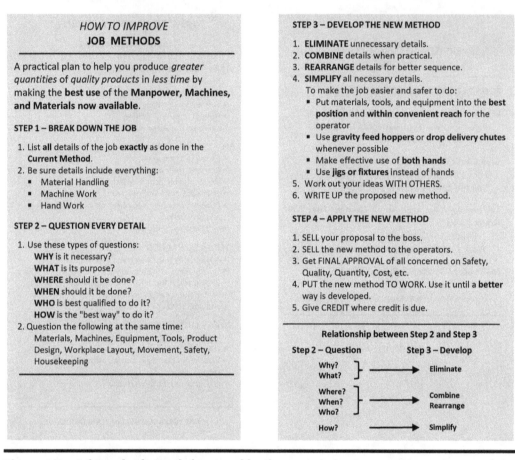

HOW TO IMPROVE
JOB METHODS

A practical plan to help you produce *greater quantities* of *quality products* in *less time* by making the **best use** of the **Manpower, Machines, and Materials now available**.

STEP 1 – BREAK DOWN THE JOB

1. List **all** details of the job **exactly** as done in the **Current Method**.
2. Be sure details include everything:
   ■ Material Handling
   ■ Machine Work
   ■ Hand Work

STEP 2 – QUESTION EVERY DETAIL

1. Use these types of questions:
   WHY is it necessary?
   WHAT is its purpose?
   WHERE should it be done?
   WHEN should it be done?
   WHO is best qualified to do it?
   HOW is the "best way" to do it?
2. Question the following at the same time:
   Materials, Machines, Equipment, Tools, Product Design, Workplace Layout, Movement, Safety, Housekeeping

STEP 3 – DEVELOP THE NEW METHOD

1. **ELIMINATE** unnecessary details.
2. **COMBINE** details when practical.
3. **REARRANGE** details for better sequence.
4. **SIMPLIFY** all necessary details.
   To make the job easier and safer to do:
   ■ Put materials, tools, and equipment into the **best position** and **within convenient reach** for the operator
   ■ Use **gravity feed hoppers** or **drop delivery chutes** whenever possible
   ■ Make effective use of **both hands**
   ■ Use **jigs or fixtures** instead of hands
5. Work out your ideas WITH OTHERS.
6. WRITE UP the proposed new method.

STEP 4 – APPLY THE NEW METHOD

1. SELL your proposal to the boss.
2. SELL the new method to the operators.
3. Get FINAL APPROVAL of all concerned on Safety, Quality, Quantity, Cost, etc.
4. PUT the new method TO WORK. Use it until a **better** way is developed.
5. Give CREDIT where credit is due.

Relationship between Step 2 and Step 3

Step 2 – Question	Step 3 – Develop
Why? What? } →	Eliminate
Where? When? Who? } →	Combine Rearrange
How? →	Simplify

Figure 1.8   Job Methods Card, front and back

TWI, Lean, and Kata

Because TWI was introduced into Japan in the early 1950s, just after the war when the concepts of Lean, as embodied in the TPS, were still in their formative stages, it is not surprising to see the strong influence TWI has had on Japanese business practices and the cultural patterns Rother observed when he studied Toyota decades later. When we think of the three core concepts of Lean – Respect for People, Standardized Work, and Continuous Improvement – we can see the direct correlation to the original three TWI methods. Job Relations laid the foundation for respecting people, building strong relationships through treating people as individuals, and listening and responding to their opinions and feelings. Job Instruction was a critical piece, as we will see in Chapter 6, in helping Toyota achieve its goal of attaining standardized work by giving production leaders both a way of writing the standards down and a way of disseminating standard processes to multiple people at multiple sites. Job Methods, as we've pointed out, was not only a core element in the advent of kaizen, but also introduced the Japanese to proposal systems that became one of the strongest elements of Japanese management systems.[20]

As a side note, now that we know what the word *kata* means in Japanese, the original names for the TWI programs in Japanese all used the suffix, *kata*. Job Instruction was called *Shigoto no Oshie-kata*, or The Way to Teach Jobs. Job Relations was called *Hito no Atsukai-kata*, or The Way to Handle People. Job Methods was called *Kaizen no Shi-kata*, or The Way to do Kaizen. When Rother looked at the Toyota patterns of management and called them *Kata*, he was following a long Japanese tradition of using methods, or patterns, of practice that are embodied in all the arts, most famously the martial arts. It would be natural, then, for the Japanese to embrace the TWI methodologies as they were presented to them in this pattern by the Americans. That is surely the reason these TWI skills were maintained until this day in Japan in their original form.

The Components Must Play Well Together

In selecting the correct pieces to put into a management system, it is imperative that these components work well together. Remember, the value of the system is greater than the sum of its parts because the individual parts, by themselves, add no value outside of what the whole system is trying to accomplish. The running joke about buying a Jaguar back in the early 1990s was that you had to buy two, one for spare parts. The reason was that the parts did not work well together and the car would break down when they failed. On the other hand, when your components "play well together" and support each other synergistically, exceptional things begin to happen, and we begin to get a glimpse of what it might be like to become an organization that stands head and shoulders above the competition.

The rest of this book will be devoted to showing how to develop this synergy in the management system. As an example, let's examine our three TWI modules – Job Instruction, Job Relations, and Job Methods – and see how they interact well together as a sub-system of the overall system.

---

[20] Alan G. Robinson and Dean M. Schroeder, "Training, Continuous Improvement, and Human Relations: The U.S. TWI Programs and the Japanese Management Style," *California Management Review* (Winter 1993).

Even if you introduce a good training method like JI into your organization, you may hear supervisors say, somewhat bitterly, "But they still won't listen to me." That might be true, but it does not mean that the JI method will not work for those employees. This is not a failure of instruction but a failure of leadership. One of the points made in the Job Relations training is, "A person with no followers is not a leader." In other words, if they are not "following" your instructions (JI), then you are not "leading" (JR). JR creates skill in leading, and you will have to apply this skill first if you want your JI skill to work. Here, we can see the symbiotic relationship between JI and JR.

There are countless stories of kaizen activities that initially generated good results but were not sustained because workers fell back on their old habits. Improvements made using Job Methods (JM) are of no value if we do not have JI skill to teach people the new method effectively so that the new way quickly becomes "the way we've always done it." JI skill entails so much more than just "here is how you do it." It strives to get the person interested in doing the job by showing the importance of following the standard. It gives the reasons we do it in specific ways to convince the learners and gain acceptance. It follows up with learners to ensure they are maintaining the method without question.

Conversely, if we try to improve a process that is unstable, where everyone is doing it differently, then there will be no basis upon which to question the current method, and the "new way" will be just one more way of many, many ways that people are doing the job. Taiichi Ono, founder of the TPS, famously said, "Without standards there is no kaizen." Here, we must first apply our JI skill to stabilize the work process, building a steady current method, and then use our JM skill to study, build on, and improve this baseline. This is the symbiotic relationship between JI and JM.

Finally, one of the key tenants of the JM program is to get operators and staff involved in practicing and making the improvements. It has always been baked into the JM process from its inception. When people have a say in their work and can participate in and take ownership of the improved methods, this builds trust in the new standard and motivation to follow it. Remember, the goal of JR is to get people's dedication and cooperation in doing the work. Participating in the use of JM directly affects JR, and the two skills feed off each other. Relationships built on trust through JR, in turn, inspire and motivate people to participate in the JM activity. This is the symbiotic relationship between JM and JR.

We like to characterize the TWI program as a "three-legged-stool." If you take away one leg, it cannot stand. This represents the inter-relationships between the skills summed up in Figure 1.9.

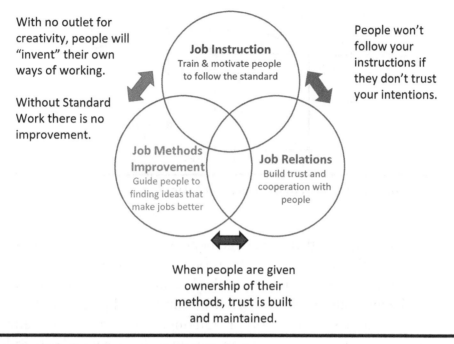

Figure 1.9   Relationship among 3 TWI Methods

Integrated Model of a Management System

You might be thinking, with all this talk of system components and meta-processes, aren't things like Leader Standard Work, Visual Controls, and Daily Accountability Process, the three elements of Mann's Lean Management System, meta-processes in themselves? The answer is certainly yes. In that case, is there a hierarchy to all these meta-processes, and if so, does it really, in the end, even matter? Remember what we pointed out in the Introduction, "All models are wrong, but some are useful." The Gear Train Model, while it does an excellent job of showing how components must work well together, portrays a hierarchical system of cascading gears, from big to small, which may not be as useful for us here because these meta-processes work, as we just saw with the TWI components, next to each other without one directing or controlling the other. So, a "more useful" model might be something like we see in Figure 1.10 where each component of the management system is like a corner of a cube and relates equally with any other corner at any given time.

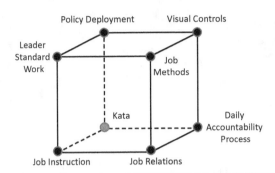

Figure 1.10   Integrated Model of Management System

What we see, then, is that a management system is **not** necessarily a *parallel* system that runs next to the production/patient care/service system, but an *integrated* system of multiple components that function *inter*dependently at all times. This would mean that all people in the organization, regardless of position or "ranking," could be actively engaged in any, or all, management system components whether they be high level meta-processes or practical process tools.

The traditional model of management has the higher-level "thinkers" of the organization doing the control work of the system while the lower-level "doers" carry out the instructions of said control system. But what about having the front-line people think about and control their own work? Don't they really know much more about the content of that work because they do it every day and, therefore, have more and better ideas on how to do it better? That fundamentally changes their role but, more significantly, puts into question the traditional role of management. Much of the rest of this book will address what that changed role might be, but for now let's just say that management must act more as coaches guiding the control work as it is carried out on the front lines, rather than controllers telling those front-line people what to do.

Even though you might be called a manager or a supervisor, who should be managing or supervising the work and not actually doing it, the reality is that supervisory staff in a plant or hospital or service center might be called "working leads." They are participating with their people in getting the work done. At the end of the day, no one in the organization should be divorced from the direct work of providing value to the customers. Disney, which is so good at management that it runs a school of management in Orlando, likes to portray everyone's job at the theme parks as a "performance" and stresses the putting on of a "show" for the customers every day all day long. One day, a janitor spied a group of executives touring the park and saw them casually walk by some trash on the ground without picking it up and throwing it away. The janitor ran up to one of the men in suits, tapped him on the shoulder, and, pointing his finger accusingly, said to him, "Bad show!" That is what Disney tells its people when they have done a poor job. Whether you are a janitor or an executive, you are responsible for providing value to the customer.

A similar example involves a high-level Toyota executive from Japan seen touring a dealership in the United States. As the group went through the repair shop, the executive noticed a mechanic under the hood of a vehicle who was obviously struggling with a repair. The well-dressed visitor in the expensive suit threw off his jacket, rolled up his sleeves, tucked his tie into his shirt, and got right next to the mechanic under the hood, asking what the problem was. He wanted to find out what they could do better in designing and building the car so that mechanics would have fewer difficulties with repairs. More than just that, though, it was a vivid display of the working culture where everyone is equal and *inter*dependent in providing value to the customer.

So far so good. It's not too difficult to understand how members of management can be active in front-line processes and work, at least to the level their skills allow, right alongside the other employees.[21] But what about management taking directions from the staff? That's a bigger shift. In our Kata work at hospitals, and we do this intentionally, we literally have front-line staff act as coaches while learners are members of management, even top executives. No kidding! And guess what? Management people love it because they can begin to "practice what they preach" in front of the workforce and learn from the incredible experiences these front-line people have to offer them. On the one hand, the experienced front-line coaches are not telling their management learners how to do their jobs (just as they do not want to be told by management how to do their jobs) but are coaching them on how to do these jobs better. On the other hand, the management learners are making use of practical tools, things like kaizen, 5S, cause-and-effect diagrams, 5 Whys, etc., to make their work as managers more productive. It's a real role reversal that changes the dynamic of the how people see and treat each other in the organization.

Each employee plays a pre-defined role in any organization, and these roles are categorized in importance by things like titles, salary levels, bonuses, office space, parking spots, segregate lounges, etc. Whether these

---

[21] We understand the fact that some plants have union rules by which management is expressly forbidden to do any work done by union members. These rules must be followed when they are present.

parameters, especially pay levels, are set fairly and equitably is not a question we could possibly answer. No employee, at any level, will ever be fully satisfied with his or her compensation – it will never be enough. These levels, in the aggregate, are ultimately dictated by society, how each role is valued on a supply-and-demand basis. However, what we can do is question and change how we see and how we treat each other, and this will affect the way our management system works, for better or worse. For example, a Toyota subsidiary we visited likes to see the organization chart flipped over, an upside-down pyramid, where the workers are at the "top" of the chart, and the CEO is at the "bottom." Just because one person's role has traditionally been seen as higher, or lower, does not mean we cannot re-imagine the hierarchy, regardless of how society currently values each.

When we see how people at all levels and in every corner of the organization can better work as team players, we begin to conceive a more integrated model of management where everyone is a collaborator. To get this kind of deep integration, it becomes critical for people to "connect the dots" between the different pieces of the management system. Our management system model grows a bit more complex, then, like a polyhedron with many sides and corners connected to and dependent on each other (see Figure 1.11). These are

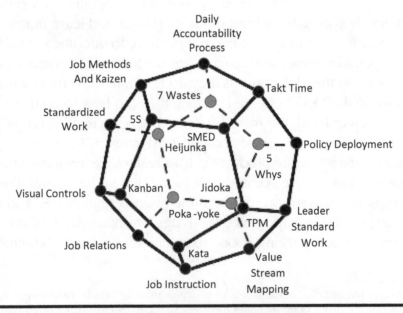

Figure 1.11 Fully Integrated Model of Management System

the pieces we have put into play and, for the remainder of this book, we'll look at how we can best "play the game" with these pieces.

Conclusion – Think Systemically

This opening chapter has looked at what pieces we should put into a management system for it to function smoothly. *Think Systemically*, one of our guiding principles, means thinking about how we operate across the entire system because what happens at any point will either improve or damage what happens in other parts of the process. To use a sports analogy, "How are we playing the game?" Do we have all the right players in the right places and are they executing their assignments properly so that, as a team, we can score the goal and win the game? You may have a hotshot quarterback, but if there are no capable blockers on the front line there won't be enough time for the receivers to get down field before the pass is thrown. It is often said that a quarterback is only as good as his offensive line. Likewise, even if your hospital has the best orthopedic surgeon in the world doing total joint replacement surgery, if the admissions staff, our front-line employees, fail to document incoming patients correctly, Medicare or the insurance companies may not reimburse you for all the great work she does in the OR. That is not winning the game.

The next chapter will continue looking at the management system from the dimension of Purpose, how we align these components so they are working together productively and effectively to achieve the goals of the organization. Part 2 will focus on the People dimension, our attitude and approach to dealing with people, and ourselves, which is vital to the success of the entire management system. Part 3 will look at Process, how we get these management system elements to work well and deliver. Part 4 will focus on sustainment and getting results.

Everything we want to present here builds on, and does not in any way replace, the work of those who have come before us. To best follow our discussion, we highly recommend the following books: David Mann's *Creating a Lean Culture: Tools to Sustain Lean Conversions*, Pascal Dennis' *Lean Production Simplified: A Plain-Language Guide to the World's Most Powerful Production System* and *Getting the Right Things Done*, Mike Rother's *Toyota Kata* and *The Toyota Kata Practice Guide*, and Patrick Graupp's *The TWI Workbook: Essential Skills for Supervisors* and *Implementing TWI: Creating and Managing a Skills-Based Culture*.

Chapter 2

How to Align the System Components

We were watching a morning safety huddle at a large hospital in the mid-South when someone said that a patient had fallen the night before. According to the Agency for Healthcare Research and Quality, a part of the U.S. Department of Health and Human Services, between 700,000 and 1,000,000 people fall each year while in the hospital, many of them elderly patients. Since 2008, Medicare and Medicaid stopped reimbursing hospitals for treating many types of hospital-acquired conditions, or "never events" (things that should *never* happen), which means that hospitals must bear the full cost of treating these injuries. Needless to say, fall prevention is a major concern of any hospital, not only for the safety and well being of its patients but for the severe financial ramifications on the institution.

The question then arises as to whether the actions we are taking on the front lines to prevent these falls are connected to and aligned with the highest-level strategic initiatives being taken around fall prevention. For that matter, is there any work being done at all at the front-line levels to prevent falls? If there is a strategic plan to reduce falls, is it being communicated effectively to those working directly with patients? And if, for example, training is carried out on how to perform specific actions or behaviors that would help prevent falls, how do we know the training has the effect we wanted? Are we sure that, with turnover and new people coming into the system, everyone is getting that training? If so, how do we ensure that these people are using the methods they were taught?

These are the kind of questions that address whether we are executing our top-line strategies effectively at the very front lines of the business. In other words, are we "connecting the dots" between what we say we want to accomplish and what we are actually doing to accomplish it? Or is there a crack in the system? A management system consists of many components, as we discussed in the last chapter, but now we need to ensure that these components are in alignment. Are the gears spinning efficiently together, or are they disengaged or slipping?

As it turned out, the nurse who reported the fall in the safety huddle said she was not aware the hospital had a comprehensive strategy to reduce falls, but she did say that she had been trained some months before on hourly patient rounding with a focus on falls prevention. In effect, she had not "connected the dots" to a larger strategy or reason she was trained and educated on the standard process. There are many reasons in the complex healthcare environment for people not being on the same page, and this certainly doesn't suggest that they are bad employees or inadequate leaders. It's not intentional. Quite the opposite: With all the competing priorities, and too many things to keep up with and learn, it's easy to see how the components of the management system are not being connected by all employees. Without understanding the value of the countermeasures put in place for fall prevention, something was missed, and the result was a patient fall.

The "Safe Room"

As we pointed out in the last chapter, Policy Deployment is an approach to comprehensively laying out top-level strategic initiatives and then guiding and coaching the implementation system, layer by layer, to each level of the organization. In a Toyota-style manufacturing environment, the very top levels of this strategic planning process will focus on topics like Safety, Quality, Delivery, and Cost. These topics can and should differ for different types of organization – manufacturing, healthcare, service, construction, finance, retail, etc. – and are influenced by the business fundamentals and objectives of the organization itself, regardless of industry. The same is true in healthcare, for example, where we focus on Quality/Safety, Delivery, Growth, and Cost (what we like to call the Four Rights – Right Care, Right Time, Right Place, Right Cost). These constitute the big headings under which all the other *hoshins* cascade.

From there you begin the process of identifying performance gaps under each of the big headings and targeting factors that are preventing you from reaching your goals. Strategies can then be drawn up for eliminating these factors, and the whole planning process, based on these higher-level strategies, can be regenerated at each level of the enterprise. The whole project can seem overwhelming, and it is, but the goal of *Hoshin Kanri*, as Pascal Dennis portrays it, should always be on the critical few problems, the big obstacles in our path, so that we do not bog down our system with more work than it can ever hope to accomplish.[1] As Dennis likes to say, "Strategy is all about what you are saying 'no' to."[2]

While Policy Deployment for us has proven very beneficial in aligning and deploying key strategies in the organizations with which we work, starting from scratch is no small task. In spite of our grandest efforts to "keep it simple," complexity immediately sets in due to the scale of the ground that needs to be covered and the difficulties in generating consistent communication and building consensus. We never cease to be amazed at how, after truly herculean efforts at overcommunication and involvement, employees at the front lines of the organization don't know or understand the reasons for the chosen goals. With so many initiatives being put into play by upper management, people fail to "connect the dots" and to understand how the whole system is supposed to work, as we saw with the nurse in the safety huddle. Ultimately, Policy Deployment, aligning the goals of the enterprise with the daily activities of frontline associates, is easy to articulate but incredibly difficult to attain.

Much of the today's management style, as we noted in the last chapter, still comes from a background shaped by a command-and-control environment where people in authority tell those without authority what to do, but not always how and why. Key elements to the success of Policy Deployment, which include good understanding, coaching, and involvement at all levels of the enterprise, are very different and counter to this traditional "top-down" management culture. In order to succeed with Policy Deployment, then, we must change the environment in order to affect that culture. One of the ways we have tried is to create what we like to call the Safe Room.

This is not a new concept. Used widely in Japan and part of the Toyota Production System, the *obeya* (literally, "large room") is the War Room, where people can meet and discuss project management. Others like to call it the Strategy Room, the Think Tank, or the Incubator. However, working in the mid-South, and with a Christian-based organization, we wanted to stay

---

[1] Pascal Dennis, *Lean Production Simplified: A Plain-Language Guide to the World's Most Powerful Production System, Third Edition* (Boca Raton, FL: CRC Press, 2016).
[2] From coaching sessions with Pascal Dennis.

away from Japanese terminology as best we could while avoiding war and violence metaphors, however appropriate they might be to some. Most of all, we wanted to designate the room a "safe" place for people to speak their minds and be transparent about their feelings without fear of intimidation or adverse ramifications. The old culture (away from which we were trying to gravitate) was an environment in which people were afraid to say what they were thinking and had ample experience to justify their fears. What we called the place, then, made a difference.

As it turns out, we were experimenting with the Safe Room concept in a hospital that had just opened a brand-new facility where there was open, undeveloped industrial space on one wing of the top floor of the building. This was advantageous because, early in the process, we were hesitant to put up information boards all over the new building thinking they would be messy and chaotic. But our process was evolving, and we knew that visual management, where people can live through pictures and stories, is a powerful means of affecting thinking patterns and behaviors. Traditional management practice has the mindset that our future paths must be well thought out beforehand and must be "correct" before they are rolled out, but we were learning, through the *Hoshin Kanri* process, that visual boards were an effective means of "showing our thinking," even if that thinking was not fully formed yet.

This was a huge shift for the organization! Instead of having the right answers, we were experimenting and learning, through our many failures, what was really happening in the organization. The availability of the industrial space gave us permission to be messy and just throw things on the walls and display our thoughts as they came up, however chaotic that might be. Here was a place where people could argue and be honest, abandoning the pretention that everything was neatly and nicely put together beforehand. In effect, the setting allowed them to step out of their mental boxes by sharing ideas that were unrefined and still developing so they could make them better through the discussions. It helped them to be creative with their thinking. It also allowed them to open their minds to other people's thinking, to be strategic as a team, with the needs of the organization.

The Safe Room became the key area for strategy deployment. This is where the top-level Policy Deployment boards live and where the hospital's leaders meet to make sure they are working on the right things and that those initiatives are flowing all the way down to the front lines where the work gets done (see Figure 2.1). The health system strategies are laid out right across the center of the room when you walk in, and anyone is welcome to come up to the room to see what is there. We even have visitors

Figure 2.1 Brad Parsons in Safe Room with CFO

come up to the room to observe meetings. It's a positive space intended to make people comfortable at any time; when there, they can't help but see the strategies on the walls and, with a glance, know where we are and where we need to be with regards to the fiscal year and the organization's goals.

The room has evolved to encompass all aspects of the management system beginning with visual representations of the principles and systems that make up the core of the management system. For our group, that means things like posters of the TWI methods and foundations along with the Five Needs Model that is at the heart of TWI practice. It's visual representations of the Kata improvement and coaching routines and a model of how we approach standardized work practice. People in the room assemble around these posters, freely discussing their thoughts and experiences with the content, before moving on to daily and weekly meetings that are also held in the Safe Room. These can be everything from the daily Safety Huddle to the Shepherding Groups that lead different hospital-wide initiatives (more on this in later chapters). Each group has its own set of posters and boards displayed in the Safe Room beside and around the strategy deployment boards. Moreover, it is simply open space for spin-off meetings and other work groups to meet because there is more white board space up there than anywhere else in the hospital. If you need time to think, to write, to draw, to compare notes, you go to the Safe Room.

The management system of this hospital is anchored in the Safe Room where all employees can meet and talk freely about organization-wide activities that begin with the top-level *hoshin* targets displayed front and center for everyone to see, read, gather around, and discuss. But this is only where the work begins. Departmental huddle boards and Kata boards, which track the activities cascading from the strategy boards, are placed in each department as these activities are focused on and carried out in each area. Alignment is only attained when these activities tie directly back to the Safe Room strategy (see Table 2.1).

Table 2.1 Cascading Priorities from Top-Line Strategy to Front-Line Deployment

LEVEL	CHART	CONTENT
Safe Room Strategy Deployment Boards	Strategic A3 (SA3)	Improve **Patient Experience** by measuring HCAHPS scores – goal to achieve a mean score of 81.0
	Status Update A3	Monthly progress on each unit's portion of specific work done to achieve goal
	Visual Run Chart	Bar graph showing actual scores vs. overall target in each domain
Departmental huddle boards (areas that impact the SA3)	Tactical A3	**Specific for each unit to <u>achieve a portion of the strategic gap,</u> based on where they have the *biggest impact* and the *largest opportunity*:**
		5West – Discharge/Nurse Communication 4West – Discharge 4East – Pain/Responsiveness of Staff 3West – Nurse Communication/Pain 3East – Nurse Communication ED – ED flow and admit/discharge time
	Visual Department Data	Same run chart as SA3 with additional bar graph showing department specific progress on area tracked above
Daily and/or weekly work	Kata Board or Idea Generation	Specific to next Target Condition. *(e.g., All nurses know discharge plan for their patients; off-going nurse communicates it at bedside shift report.)*

(Sample lines taken from various boards)

Connecting the Dots

Once the strategy has been set, activity must be initiated and carried out in order to achieve the goals set out in the planning. At this stage, traditional management practice might dictate some type of action planning or project management course of action. A more simplistic approach might be to just "hold them accountable" to implementing the required program, whoever "they" might be. As we alluded to earlier, in a command-and-control environment, bosses give orders and subordinates carry them out. This remains true today for many businesses, and many very successful businesses at that. But we have learned that a more rigorous program of engaging employees at all levels of the organization can better foster a culture of continuous improvement; we believe that a more enlightened, and we think more effective, approach is to look at not only the ends but also the means for carrying out the plans needed to achieve the goals.

Rather than forcing implementation of strategic action plans on an unwilling workforce, it would be smarter to guide and coach employees to find their own way of achieving the organization's goals. This may seem to go without saying, as most Lean practitioners understand the importance of getting employee involvement. But Lean experts also tell us that between 50 and 95% of Lean implementations fail, meaning they didn't do any better with Lean than with what they had before. This means that we are not successfully aligning our front-line activities with our professed goals. What is going wrong here?

Jerry Sternin, a former assistant dean at Harvard Business School and director of the Positive Deviance Initiative, is quoted as saying, "It's easier to act your way into a new way of thinking, than think your way into a new way of acting." In other words, simply talking at people and trying to convince them to change their behavior and performance will not be effective. Even if they "think" that you are right with what you want them to do, and for all the right reasons, just thinking they should do something will not be enough to get them to actually do it. As the Japanese like to say, "Knowing and doing are two different things." On the other hand, if you get them to start practicing some basic patterns and skills, the very "act" of doing these behaviors, and seeing with their own eyes the results they get, will change their way of thinking about what they have done. Once their thinking has been changed, the new behavior and performance will naturally follow.

We are not, in terms of "acting" our way forward, referring to specific actions we have designated in our *hoshin* planning – these will always be unique to each enterprise based on the circumstances at that period of time in their development – but the meta-processes we talked about in Chapter 1 that can be practiced and applied to any situation at any time. The secret is getting people participating in the alignment of their daily work to the organization's goals using meta-processes, routines that are foundational and can be applied to any situation, that can be learned and internalized through practice. These practices will guide them down the right paths and change how they think about the work.

There are many practices and programs that engage all levels of the workforce and can be brought into play in a management system, things like Value Stream Mapping, Kaizen, Total Quality Maintenance, A3 Problem Solving, etc. All of these are effective when put into a well-conceived system. We have found Kata practice to be a meta-process that puts front-line people in the driver's seat, so to speak, allowing them to steer their way to the organization's strategic goals. In Chapters 5 and 6, we will discuss in more detail how we use Kata to succeed in the Process dimension of a management system; here we want to focus, from the Purpose dimension, on alignment. Are we capable, using practices like Kata, of aligning the work we do on the front lines with the goals outlined in our Strategic Planning? This is what we call "connecting the dots."

Our employees, and all participants in the management system, must be able to connect the dots and understand how everything we do is interrelated in a system. For example, after over a year of introducing and applying the Job Instruction component of TWI at one large hospital, we began to introduce Job Relations. As we discussed in the last chapter, we need the leadership skills of Job Relations if we want people to follow our directions in Job Instruction. Moreover, our Kata practice at this hospital had made clear that poor relations was an *obstacle* to getting to standardized work through Job Instruction, so Job Relations was a logical next step. Knowing this, we were astonished to hear an employee say, after hearing about the upcoming Job Relations training, "Oh, that means we're done with Job Instruction, right?" The answer was an emphatic, "No!" Employees are conditioned to see new programs or initiatives as individual, separate and unrelated endeavors, the next flavor of the month, rather than components of a system that are tied together like the sub-systems of a car – the steering, brakes, engine, wheels, etc. – or the sub-systems of the human body – circulatory, digestive, respiratory, muscular, etc. In effect, they are unable to "connect the dots."

Much work is needed, then, to help people see the relationships between these pieces we put into our management system. We should not leave people on their own, even after we have tried diligently to explain how the system works, because they are not able to think their way into the desired behavior. We must coach them into acting in a way that develops the systematic thinking we need from them in order to align their work with organization goals. Once they see, for example, how good job relations smooth the way to standardized work, they will better understand and "connect the dots" between Job Instruction and Job Relations.

The components of the management system need to be in alignment; this imperative follows directly from our guiding principle to *Create Constancy of Purpose*. What needs to be aligned are (1) the top-level *strategic* goals outlined by top management leaders, (2) mid-level *tactical* goals that flow directly from the top-level planning charts but address specific action plans to be taken in individual departments, and (3) front-line *operational* assignments, projects, initiatives, etc. that are carried out by front-line employees, individually or in groups, in each specific department or value stream. We must always ask ourselves if the work we're doing on the front lines is aligned to the highest-level strategic initiatives: Is there actual work being done at the front-line levels that seeks to close those high-level gaps? This is the vertical connecting of the dots.

At the same time, we must consider the horizontal connections of work being done between departments. For example, if there is a surge in orders seen by the production department of a manufacturing facility, we may jump to the conclusion that the plant will not be able to handle the additional volume. But the truth may lie more in the interactions with other departments that work together with the plant like purchasing, warehousing, distribution, human resources, accounting, etc. If these handoffs are weak or poorly handled, the upsurge in production volume will overload the system regardless of the plant's ability to handle all the orders.

A Manufacturing Example of Alignment

It goes without saying that Safety is, and always will be, a major imperative for any manufacturing facility. "Safety First" has been a slogan for many decades now, and great strides have been achieved over that time to prevent accidents, injuries and near misses. Yet, we can never become complacent with these good results because, in spite of our best efforts, injuries and fatalities continue to occur. The safety of our employees in a dangerous working environment must always be our highest priority.

Even if safety and safety programs are highlighted at the highest levels of our strategic planning, we cannot be assured that there is alignment with these priorities at the front lines of the work. Misalignment occurs when we have competing pressures, for example, to reduce costs or get out production and meet quotas "no matter what it takes." The pressure to "make the numbers" will mean that managers, supervisors, and operators will cut corners on safe work procedures and safety protocols in order to catch up with the schedule. Worst of all, even as they profess fidelity to the safety program, management at all levels may set a tone, directly or indirectly, that the "good workers" are willing to put themselves at risk to meet the targets.

Here, alignment means not only practicing what we preach about the importance of safety, from the highest levels of responsibility to the people performing the work, but applying safety factors directly into the goals of everything else we do in the plant. When we strive to create stable work habits by standardizing work processes and procedures, we must also endeavor to find the *safe way* to do the job. When we improve the process through our kaizen efforts, we must endeavor to find a *safer way* of doing the job. Moreover, if we find ourselves continually fighting fires and trying to catch up to the schedule, our top-line strategic efforts should be directed at creating stability in our processes to take away the pressure to cut corners and short cut these very processes. In other words, standardized work and continuous improvement are foundations, not only to creating higher quality of product/service and greater efficiency of output/delivery, but to creating discipline in our daily practice, which *frees us* from the chaos of fire-fighting to focus on critical elements such as safety. In this way, safety is an integral part of everything we do.

A Healthcare Example of Alignment

In addition to the patient falls we discussed at the top of this chapter, a source of poor patient care and extreme financial hardship on a healthcare institution is when people contract illnesses while in the hospital's care. While poor hand hygiene is a major cause, and covered extensively in another work,[3] common

---

[3] Patrick Graupp and Martha Purrier, *Getting to Standard Work in Health Care: Using TWI to Create a Foundation for Quality Care* (Boca Raton, FL: CRC Press, 2013).

sources of infections are central lines and catheters inserted into a patient's body for days or weeks; they provide an opening for germs to enter the body if they are not properly maintained. These are commonly called CLABSIs (Central Line-Associated Bloodstream Infections) and CAUTIs (Catheter-Associated Urinary Tract Infections). Not only are hospitals not reimbursed for the care they must deliver for these hospital-acquired illnesses, these "never events," Medicare applies penalties that can amount to millions of dollars to hospitals for not meeting strict targets in infection control. Under the strategic headings of Quality and Cost, reduction and elimination of CLABSIs and CAUTIs is always a high priority in the Policy Deployment plan.

At the strategic planning level, the institution most likely will set a goal to reduce CLABSIs and CAUTIs. They may even target certain areas of the hospital, like the Intensive Care Unit (ICU), where a high number of central lines and catheters are used. Once they toss these aggressive goals down to the next level, in this case the ICU, the department will come up with its own goals and plans for combating infections, which will be more tactical and specific to the work done in that department. For example, they may set up training for all nurses on the unit to standardize procedures for doing Central Line Dressing Changes and Catheter Care, for which variation leads to instability in the quality of the work and provides opportunities for infections to set in (see Figure 2.2). The hypothesis would be that if every nurse did the work the same, correct way each and every time it was performed, the department could reduce infections in these areas.

In the ICU, in order to carry out and prove their hypothesis, they may set up a team with a leader assigned to plan and carry out the training (see Figure 6.10 for an example of a Training Timetable for the ICU). They may have to cooperate and coordinate with other specialties like safety and training, but they will "own" the initiative. There will be many obstacles to overcome, not the least of which will be nurses claiming to be too busy to do training and, especially for those with long service careers, feeling their way of doing the work is correct and "the best way," and that there is no need for training. The team will have to ensure it has the skills to do a proper job of instruction and be able to motivate the ICU workforce to follow the new methods taught. Moreover, it will have to create a structure for validating that work is being consistently performed to the new standard and that new people coming into the department receive and follow the training. These tasks take skill, dedication, time, and hard work to fulfill, and alignment will not be achieved if they are ignored.

JOB INSTRUCTION BREAKDOWN SHEET - HEALTHCARE

Task: <u>Central Line and PICC Dressing Change</u>

Supplies: <u>Clean gloves, dressing kit, CHG dressing, sterile saline syringes</u>

Equipment & Materials: <u>Trash can, bedside table</u>
- HAND HYGIENE (HH)

IMPORTANT STEPS	KEY POINTS	REASONS
A logical segment of the operation when something happens to advance the work.	Anything in a step that might – 1. Make or break the job 2. Injure the worker 3. Make the work easier to do (i.e., "knack", "trick", special timing, bit of special information)	Reasons for key points
1. Prepare room & patient	1. Prepare table and patient 2. In bed on back 3. Elevate bed 4. Masks 5. HH before gloves	1. Safety and decrease risk of infection 2. More stability, avoid line displacement 3. Good body mechanics 4. & 5. Decrease risk of infection
2. Remove and inspect site	1. Slowly toward insertion site 2. Squirt saline on CHG gel; don't touch 3. Assess for infection 4. Look & feel	1. Avoid line displacement 2. Loosens gel to come off more easily, skin integrity 3. Decrease risk of infection 4. Identify and treat infection
3. Clean with alcohol	1. HH/don sterile gloves 2. No alcohol on the PICC catheter 3. From insertion site outwards 4. 3 sticks to 3 inches 5. Air dry	1. Decrease risk of infection 2. Prevent breakdown of PICC catheter 3. Clean contaminants away from insertion site 4. Removes biofilm 5. Dry time is kill time
4. Disinfect w/CHG	1. If prevantics-flat side to skin/both sides If chloraprep-squeeze wings 2. Back & forth to 3" from site 3. Air Dry 30 sec	1. Correct Chg. Distribution, decrease risk of infection 2. Clean both sides of the epithelial cells 3. Dry time is kill time
4. Apply new dressing	1. Holding by handles 2. Gel pad over site 3. Notch over tubing 4. Smooth surface to edges 5. Change hep-locks with green caps	1. Prevents contamination of dressing 2. Provides continuous antimicrobial action 3. Seals dressing 4. Avoids air bubbles or wrinkles 5. Decreases infection risk
6. Label dressing	1. Remove PPE/HH 2. Date/time dressing 3. Lower bed 4. Document in EMR	1. & 2. Decrease risk of infection 2. Communicates with Care team 3. Patient Safety 4. Communicates with Care team

Figure 2.2 Job Instruction Breakdown Sheet for Central Line Dressing Change

Aligning the Components – the Gear Train Model Revisited

In the Introduction, we talked about a management system being like a gear train in which different elements of the management system interact like interconnected gears spinning together, either smoothly and efficiently or out of synch with some gears disengaged and others scraping along together due to lack of lubrication or poor design. Now that we've made a basic representation of what the Policy Deployment, or *Hoshin Kanri*, process looks like, let's see how it can be described by our Gear Train Model using the example of the hospital in which we set up the Safe Room. We have found that using this Gear Model succeeds in getting people across all parts of the organization to understand how a management system works.

At the top level, we have our strategic planning process: We lay out yearly goals into what we could call our "true north" strategy statements (see Figure 2.3). On our boards, under each one of the main categories of Right Care, Right Time, Right Place, and Right Cost, we have one or more columns of documents, starting with a Strategic Deployment A3, each representing a strategic gap that needs to be filled. In each Strategic A3, or "Mother A3," there will be a statement of the gap, a reflection section describing the situation, and then a set of hypotheses, the if-then statements of the scientific

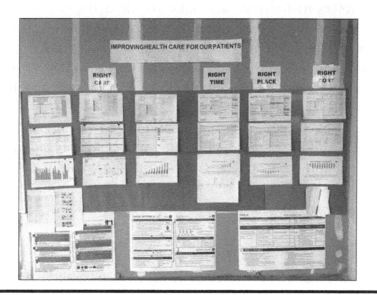

Figure 2.3   Policy Deployment Board

method, that suggest ideas for closing the gap. Attached to these will be plans for the fiscal year along with back-up plans and follow-up plans for carrying out the projects. Table 2.2 shows the detailed guidance we use for documenting the Strategic A3. Finally, there will be a status A3, a summary table of activities from the Strategic A3 (see Table 2.3), and a list of metrics that can be reviewed in regular meetings of the team.

This activity can be seen as the biggest gear in our Gear Model; the senior leadership team will meet monthly to keep abreast of progress throughout the year (see Figure 2.4). For each strategy, a Key Thought Leader is assigned responsibility for leading the gap-closing activity all the way to the front lines. At monthly meetings, the Thought Leaders will lead a discussion in which the whole team studies and adjusts the processes while reviewing the current metrics. That does not mean there is no activity between these meetings. Visiting the different areas supporting the closure of the gap, the leadership team will "play catch ball" with the local staff to review progress and make needed adjustments. In "catch ball," rather than simply telling people what to do, leaders communicate back and forth with staff at each level and across levels giving their requests and suggestions while getting ideas and feedback until consensus is reached. In effect, they are doing PDSA[4] at the highest level.

WHAT IS CATCH BALL?

Catch Ball refers to the give and take required between management levels and staff during the planning and implementation process embodied in Policy Deployment. This entails frank, reality-based discussions between and within levels of management. Catch Ball is not a one-time activity but an integral part of both the development and life of the Policy Deployment process. By using Catch Ball:

■ strategies and tactics cascade throughout the organization.
■ the vision and daily activities of the front-line team members are linked together.
■ we validate, align, and cascade our way of thinking.

---

[5] Plan-Do-Study-Act, referred to more traditionally as PDCA, Plan-Do-Check-Act. We prefer the verb Study to Check since it implies learning and growth rather than a fixed set of expectations. We also like to refer to the Act verb as Adjust, for the same reasons.

Playing Catch Ball between management levels and staff follows the logic that we should not simply tell people what to do because that closes their minds and cuts us off from access to their deep well of experience, knowledge, and creativity. If we constantly tell people what to do, in effect we are teaching them to do nothing until instructed otherwise and they never take ownership of their work. We can, however, tell people what gaps we are trying to close and make them responsible for developing strategic imperatives to support the plan. Moreover, we can give them authority to carry out their initiatives. The leader's role becomes to provide follow-up and support for success as they rely on the knowledge and ability of team members to create and enact their plans.

This process requires a different kind of leadership based on mutual trust. The team must trust the leader's judgment in picking focus areas and goals, but it is encouraged to push back with facts. That is the "catch ball" – tossing the ball back and forth. Leaders must trust their team members' ability to create and carry the plans forward. Catch Ball ensures that we are all on the same page.

At the next level, we have huddle boards in each department; they are like mini versions of the Safe Room in which local teams have weekly, rather than monthly, meetings (see Figure 2.5). The boards have the same main categories, but the department may not be working on projects under each heading. Depending on what gaps they and the senior leader in their department have decided need to be addressed, they will be following a Tactical A3, or "Baby A3," rather than the Strategic A3. The two forms follow the pattern laid out in Table 2.2. They also have a status A3 and a set of metrics, just like in the Safe Room. In the weekly meetings, the Thought Leader in charge of that strategy addresses gaps, the initiatives being run to counter those gaps, and the adjustments needed to keep progress moving forward.

In our Gear Model, we can visualize the single large gear at the top spinning all the second-level gears in unison (see Figure 2.6).

The next, or third, level is the daily activity to close the tactical gap. The best example of daily activity is the Kata Storyboard (see Figure 2.7). Following Kata practice each day, a coach reviews a learner's long-term challenge and near-term target condition as she "experiments forward" toward these goals. This challenge comes from and is directly connected to

Table 2.2   Strategic Deployment A3 Instructions

STRATEGIC DEPLOYMENT A3 — Plan

① PERFORMANCE, GAPS, CHALLENGE - IMPACT

1. What is the GAP that must be closed between the Current Condition and the Challenge?
   a. What is the one result metric (lagging metric) that defines the GAP? Make it measurable by $, %, #. Is the metric deployable? If possible, show past 3-5 year history.
   b. "What is Actually Happening (WAH)" versus "What Should be Happening (WSH)" is what defines the GAP.
   c. Be consistent and avoid confusion. For example, if the GAP is stated as dollars, try to use dollars to describe "What is Actually Happening (WAH)" versus "What Should be Happening (WSH)." Sometimes people will jump from dollars to time or some other metric. So be consistent as you progress throughout the A3.
   d. Can you SHOW visually using charts, graphs, maps, etc.?
2. What is the IMPACT? Provide an impact statement describing the impact to the Patient, Hospital, Clinic, and Employee.

This section will guide, inform, and influence ALL remaining sections. You are trying to get sponsorship in this area.

Challenge (a strategic imperative) or What Should be Happening

GAP

Current Condition or What is Actually Happening

Catch Ball

② REFLECTION ON RECENT ACTIVITIES AFFECTING THE GAP

1. The purpose of this section is to determine if activities last year had an impact, yes or no. Therefore, should we do more of that activity or something different?
2. Rate each previous year's activity either Green (G) or Red (R) based on target vs. actual results. Avoid using yellow.
3. Get stakeholders and potential stakeholders together.
4. What did you expect from the activity? What actually happened? What did you learn?
5. In addition to wins and losses we can reflect on and list resource constraints.
6. If you are stating obstacles, avoid being vague and be specific.
7. If this is an entirely new activity, then state that as the case.

Example:

ACTIVITY	RATING	KEY RESULTS/OBSTACLES
Engaged admissions staff identified and created countermeasures for loss revenue	●	Target = $1 M, Actual = $2 M, Saved = $1 M

Catch Ball

③ HYPOTHESES (IF/THEN) FOR THIS YEAR'S ACTIVITIES

1. The hypotheses are worded in an "If/Then" statement.
2. Both number and prioritize your hypotheses.
3. Ideally, the sum of these hypotheses should equal your GAP. If not, address what you know.
4. Ideally, build the hypotheses so they are 20% over your GAP.
5. You are addressing big obstacles.
6. Predict the portion that each hypothesis statement will contribute to closing the GAP.

Example: If we reduce overtime by 20% then we can deliver $200K to the bottom line (200K).

Quantify the hypothesis and then you enable the Leader Standard Work.

Catch Ball

Do

④ THIS YEAR'S ACTION PLAN (ROLL-UP OF SUBORDINATE PLANS)

1. The hypothesis should be the heading of your Goal section. So if one has five hypothesis statements then they should have five goals.
2. Need to determine how much each action will contribute to the Goal. No more than five activities.
3. Both number and prioritize your Goal section. This is similar to the Hypotheses section.
4. We are pulling versus pushing by way of Catch Ball the activities from the Tactical (Baby) A3's.
5. The "activities" are the main pieces of the supporting Tactical (Baby) A3's.
6. Ensure time schedule is layered out logically so one can see cause and effect.

If one is developing a Tactical (Baby) A3 that is supporting a Strategic (Mother) A3, it will be similar in format.

A Tactical (Baby) A3 may be addressing goals in more than one Strategic (Mother) A3.

Right Car   Right Team   Right Place   Right Cost

Right Plan

Strategic (Mother) A3

Tactical (Baby) A3

Example:

GOAL		ACTIVITIES	WHO	SCHEDULE
				O N D J F M A M J J A S
Reduce Falls from 50 to 25 incidents.	1.	Visual ID High Risk patient's room + individual (-10)	John D.	
	2.	Use bed alarms on patients ≥ 65 between the hours of 21:00 – 07:00 (-10)	Jane S.	ONGOING
	3.	One-on-one education of each patient at the bedside regarding falls & prevention (-5)	Rick F.	ONGOING

Catch Ball

STUDY, ADJUST

⑤ HOW YOU WILL FOLLOW UP

1. What are you going to do to ensure success? What might go wrong and how will you address it?
2. At what cadence will you meet with the owners of the Tactical (Baby) A3's that are contributing to this Strategic (Mother) A3?
3. When reviewing the status of activities from the Tactical (Baby) A3's some possible questions are as follows:
   a. Is the new process in place as designed? Is it on schedule? Is it looking capable? Is it trending toward the intended results? If not, why not? What is working well? What obstacles are getting in the way? Avoid being vague and be specific.
   b. What was your last step? What did you expect? What actually happened?
   c. What did you learn? What is your next step? What do you expect?

Catch Ball

Table 2.3 Status A3 Instructions

STATUS A3

OVERVIEW	TARGET	ACTUAL	COMMENTS
This is a general overview of the strategy being reviewed. This is the **GAP** that is being closed. You are describing the overall approach and results. This area relates back to the top left box plus the hypotheses on the Strategic (Mother) A3. What is the overall story?		This is based on year to date	This is the connection between what was planned, what was expected, what actually happened, and what we are learning. This helps put everything below in context.

GOAL	ACTIVITIES	PROCESS METRIC	YTD RESULTS		COMMENTS	NEXT STEPS
			TARGET	ACTUAL		
Should be taken from right side of A3. If you are in the 1st quarter and only 3 of the 5 goals are addressed in this quarter then only those 3 should be on this Status A3, not all 5.	Should be taken from right side of A3. For Strategic A3 you may only have the "Activities" column. This section should provide evidence of rounding with subordinate groups and playing Catch Ball.	Is the process in place as designed? Is it on schedule? Is it looking capable?	Is it trending toward the intended results?		If not, why not? What is working well? What is getting in the way? What are you learning? This area will also be used to communicate the relationship between plan and results that lead to next steps.	If results are being achieved, what can be done to hardwire process? If not, what needs to be adjusted?
Example: **Reduce Falls from 50 to 25 incidents.**	1. Visual ID High Risk patient's room + individual (-10)	1. Audit Tools; K-card review	(-5)	(-6)	1. We are concerned with visual fatigue of the visual aids.	?
	2. Use bed alarms on patients ≥ 65 between the hours of 21:00 — 07:00 (-10)	% of bed alarms	(-5)	(-4)	2. Initially the trial group only included surgery patients who did not have a high number of falls.	Include all patients.
	3. One-on-one education of each patient at the bedside regarding falls & prevention (-5)	% of patients educated	(-3)	(0)	3. Initially the family is being educated but then various members change and new family members were not educated.	?

the department huddle board that, as we just saw, is connected to the Safe Room. As we noted in the previous section, the regular practice of *doing* Kata at this level affects and transforms people's *thinking* about their work, not only at the storyboard but in any aspect of their day. In other planning meetings as well as in regular working conversations, it is normal to hear the Kata routine questions and expressions as people's thinking patterns evolve toward what the Japanese like to call a "problem consciousness." Here, then, with the meta-process of Kata, we begin seeing real alignment between front-line activities and organizational goals because employees take ownership of their ideas for work improvement, now strategically organized through the Kata discipline.

In our Gear Train Model, we see the third-level gears turning, but now in true synchronization with the overall system rather than spinning on their own unaware of how and why they are contributing to the larger good (see Figure 2.8). Remember our nurse in the safety huddle, who was given training on room rounding but didn't know that the reason for the training was to reduce the number and cost of falls? With Kata, targets are reconfirmed daily and aligned to the bigger challenges that are, in themselves, directed at the higher tactical goals of the department, which are targeted at achieving the overall strategic goals of the organization. The activities front-line employees are pursuing are now in close alignment with the overall management system.

Figure 2.4   Gear Train Model at the Highest Level

Figure 2.5   Departmental Huddle

Figure 2.6   Gear Train Model at Second Level

Figure 2.7   Kata Coaching Session

Figure 2.8   Gear Train Model at Third Level

The smallest gears in our model, the fourth level, represent the TWI skills deployed to overcome obstacles found in the Kata process (see Figure 2.9). For example, if an obstacle to achieving a target is the lack of standardized work, then our use of Job Instruction skill can be applied to train people to the standard, overcoming the obstacle preventing us from getting to our target condition. Earlier, we saw training used to overcome the obstacle of variation in work processes, which was keeping us from our goal of reducing in-hospital infections. More often than not, though, people problems and personality situations get in the way and prevent us from reaching our goals. For these obstacles, we can apply our Job Relations skill. When the obstacle is a poor or unsafe work process, the application of Job Methods can help us understand more clearly our current condition and generate ideas for improving the process in a way that allows us to achieve our target condition. (We will look in more detail at how Kata and TWI interact with each other in Chapter 6.)

This portrayal of the Gear Train Model shows application of the Policy Deployment (*Hoshin Kanri)*, Kata, and TWI methodologies to a management system, but, as we have said repeatedly, it is not necessary to apply these particular programs. We use them as examples because this has been our experience and we can explain how it worked for us. But with whatever

Figure 2.9   Gear Train Model at the Lowest Level

pieces you choose to deploy in your management system, the key will be integrating them into a seamless series of interconnected parts that function together as a system. This alignment *will Create Constancy of Purpose*, one of the 10 principles we are striving to follow, and one of the three corners of our management system model – Purpose, People and Process. The remainder of this book will try to show how to pursue excellence from the People as well as the Process dimensions, the other two corners of our model.

Conclusion – Top Management Involvement

Finally, it cannot be overstressed that for alignment to take place over a whole management system, active support and involvement must come from the very highest levels of the organization. In all aspects of life, whether business, social, political, or religious, we have found it to be truly amazing the ways in which the attitudes and behavior of the top leaders of any enterprise directly influence attitudes and behavior at the front lines of the organizations they lead. In effect, these top leaders really do create, and oftentimes distort, the cultures they seek to influence. How they lead makes all the difference; it will dictate the degree to which their organization is truly aligned to the goals they seek to achieve. We believe that all leaders can influence change in their areas of responsibility by acknowledging principles and their role in the management system that the team or unit uses to get results.

We have seen in this chapter the importance of "connecting the dots" so that employees at all levels of the organization, from bottom to top, are on the same page, singing from the same hymn book, rowing in the same direction, on the same wavelength, … . you get the idea. As we saw, this is not an easy task. It takes a tremendous and continuous effort. Only with this effort will you be able to get alignment and live by the principle of *Create Constancy of Purpose*.

So, what is your management system? Have you thought about the elements that your organization has put into play? How does your management system work? Is everyone connecting the dots for these activities? Whether you know it or not, your organization does have a management system, but it may not be working cohesively and with purpose. Try now to look at your own organization's efforts; see how you might "tune up" your engine so that all the parts are operating smoothly in alignment with each other.

Leading People

2

Chapter 3

How We Treat People

In Part 1, we talked about putting the right pieces for our management system into place and making sure they are in alignment and "engaged" in a way that all the gears in the gear train are spinning efficiently in unison, from top to bottom. We haven't yet talked about one of the most important parts, maybe *the* most important part, of a powerful gear train – not the gears or the shafts or the clutches, but the part you don't see, the lubrication. Why do you change the oil in your car? It's a very basic task every car owner must monitor. The engine has many moving parts that rub up against each other causing friction and heat. The oil lubricates these parts and absorbs heat, allowing the engine to run smoothly by preventing overheating and excessive wear and tear. The engine oil breaks down over time and loses its effectiveness at lubricating and absorbing heat. The oil also gets dirty, and these dirt particles cause additional damage to the parts. If you want your car to continue taking you to the places you need to go each and every day, you had better change the oil regularly before the engine breaks down.

We suggested in our Gear Train Model that strong human relations is like the "lubrication" of the management system, essential to keeping our system components in good working condition and preventing the entire system from "overheating" and breaking down. True to the model, this is also "the part you don't see." How can that be? Numerous people in a business or enterprise work together on tasks that only human beings can accomplish. But when we consider human resource systems, we look at things like job descriptions and assignments, pay scales and promotions, capacity charts, skills training and development, career development tracks, span of control, motivational programs, onboarding, and retention. All of these systems are seen from the aspect of the work we want people to do, their individual roles in the bigger scheme of what the organization is trying to accomplish. These systems are the gears, not the lubrication.

Do we ever really think about how people are getting along with each other, individually, as unique human beings? Do we take into consideration how they manage their personal lives and how that affects their work? What are the "systems" that take into account human feelings like jealousy, intimidation, narcissism, fear, or hatred? A typical business attitude is "Leave your personal problems at home," but is that possible? When we do consider "human relationships" issues, it is usually from the negative aspect of dealing with "problem employees" and the policies and rules around responding to bad behavior. Do we ask where bad behavior comes from or talk about the negative effects that stem from throwing "a monkey-wrench into the system"? On the other hand, when people smile and nod their heads as if in agreement with everything that is said and done, which is also quite typical in working environments, do we have a way of digging down with them to the deeper reality that they are simply "going along to get along" and are not really, in any way, committing to doing what they are agreeing with?

Many managers in organizations believe that these human relations issues do not apply to them in "*my* department" because "*my* people are ALL-STARS." That may be the case, and they may be very effective leaders with their own teams, but when you start to probe into their relationships with their counterparts in other departments, they are quick to complain, often-times quite bitterly, about the ramifications of the poor relations there and how this adversely affects their own work. Remember that in a production plant, product flows through other departments; your relationships with them, as well as with off-line staff functions like HR, quality, engineering, safety, etc., directly affect the success of the work in your department. In a hospital, the patients (i.e., the customers) travel through the hospital system horizontally, not vertically, as they are passed from one department to the next. They look at and judge the hospital as a whole, not by the treatment they get in any one department.

Remember our example of a principle from Chapter 1: *Mutual relationships only survive when there is mutual benefit*. This principle requires that we maintain strong relationships in which respect and trust are built among all individuals so that the Golden Rule is maintained and we thrive as a team, not just as individuals. In practicing Kata, Mike Rother points out "the coach/learner *relationship* (our italics) is at the root of the Improvement Kata approach to developing a scientific thinking mindset."[1] Here, as well, the work starts with and depends on the relationship, the foundation for everything else to succeed. When we don't possess the skills to manage human relations well, our management system struggles to function smoothly regardless of how well conceived and constructed it may be. When we don't take the time to continuously attend to human issues, the system overheats and breaks down. Here is an actual example of what that friction looks like and how it can break down the system.

The Barbara Problem – Part 1

A unit manager in a large city hospital in the mid-South received a disciplinary report on Barbara, a new Patient Care Assistant (PCA) who was still within her 90-day probation period. The report came from Sally, the Registered Nurse (RN) who had been supervising Barbara's work the day before and stated that Barbara had repeatedly failed to answer her Voalte phone,[2] refused assignments, and was disrespectful in front of patients. These were serious allegations that could easily lead to disciplinary actions.

On the day in question, Sally and Barbara were assigned patients in rooms 6 to 14. While Sally was in the middle of administering the 9 AM medications to the patient in room 7, the patient requested to sit in the chair after using the bathroom. Sally said she would get help and instructed him to wait in the bed. She stepped outside the room and called Barbara on her Voalte phone, but it went to voice mail. She started preparing the meds for room 9 and called again with the same outcome. When she went into room 9, she saw Barbara bathing the patient there. Sally told Barbara to go next door right away to assist the patient in room 7 up to the bathroom and get him in the chair and then she could come back and finish the bathing after Sally was done giving meds. Barbara replied that she was almost done and suggested Sally wait a few minutes on giving the meds and help the patient in room 7 on her own. Sally cut her off saying she was the RN and asked her to step outside to the hallway.

As soon as Barbara emerged from the room Sally, who was waiting, shouted,

---

[1] Mike Rother, *The Toyota Kata Practice Guide* (New York: McGraw-Hill Education, 2018).
[2] Clinical communication device.

Barbara, you were wrong to tell me what to do in front of the patient. The RN is in charge and I am the RN and you are the PCA. I delegate to you and you should respect that. I find your pushiness out of line and offensive. I tried to call you twice, but you refused to answer the phone. I am in the middle of administering medications and I should not stop and be distracted by doing *your* work.

Barbara responded, "I *didn't* refuse to answer. I was almost finished giving a bath which was very important to the patient before her family arrived and I wasn't trying to be pushy, I was trying to find a solution to … "
Sally cut her off saying,

This isn't the first time I have seen this behavior from you. You have not answered my calls before. So, you think that my plan is wrong. Well, let me tell you that is not your role. I am the RN – I worked hard to get my degree. Maybe you should go back to school and get your RN if you want to be in charge.

As Barbara turned to walk away, Sally added, "I'm not going to let this slide, I think your behavior could be insubordination."

Respect for People

Several things are happening in this story, but at the core of the conflict is the relationship between Sally and Barbara and the friction caused by their attitudes toward each other and their roles. These attitudes are, in the end, unrelated to the importance of giving a bath versus giving a medication. It's a personal conflict between the two employees. This is a common example of why we need to use principles to guide our way through trying situations. When we understand principles, we can better know and foresee the consequences of our actions and are, hence, more likely to make better choices. In other words, principles determine the outcomes of our actions, and the more we make choices following these principles the better the outcomes will be. A principle of effective leadership that applies here is *Respect Every Individual* (one of the ten guiding principles).

It is easy to say that we respect our fellow human beings, and most people would hesitate to say that they do not. How do we demonstrate this belief in daily life? How do we "walk the talk"? For example, do we take the time to listen to others' feelings and opinions and truly understand them without judgment or bias before we jump in and insist on our own point of view? In other words, do we *respect* the other person's standing regardless of our own position? This is not an easy thing to do and takes real skill to practice on a regular basis.

Respect starts with understanding people as individuals. Many of us unconsciously resist this, and we may hold the mistaken view that "understanding" implies "agreement." We are afraid to say, "Son, I understand why you punched your sister in the nose," because we believe that sends the message that we agree with what he did. Yet the only true way to teach him a different behavior is to understand where the bad behavior came from and work on changing the cause (anger) and not just the symptom (violence). *Empathy* means we "feel what you feel." This is different from *sympathy*, which implies a "harmony of or agreement in feeling." When we *empathize* with someone's actions or opinions, we respect the person's standing as a human being even if it does not align with who we are or what we feel we represent. Being able to understand this difference shows respect for that individual.

Respect for people leads to valuing their inherent worth and potential while working diligently to guide them toward bringing their unique contribution to the organization. When people feel respected, when they feel "understood," then they will be more ready and willing to give not only their hands but also their minds and their hearts to the work. Moreover, how we treat any one individual sends ripple effects throughout the organization as other people can see our behavior and anticipate how they, in turn, will be treated by the system. Treating people with respect, then, must come first. It is the foundation of true empowerment and the beginning of effective innovation and improvement, which we will see in Part 3 when we look at Process.

The Barbara Problem – Part 2

In a typical business scenario, the report given by Sally on Barbara's refusal to follow orders, the so-called "insubordination," may have been enough cause to dismiss her, especially considering she was still within her 90-day probation period when it is still relatively easy to get rid of a "bad apple." While most large organizations have some type of progressive disciplinary system in which an employee must first get a series of warnings, verbal and written, before he or she can be fired, insubordination is typically one of those "no tolerance" violations, which made Sally's final threat to Barbara all the more biting. But, remember, we pointed out that the lubrication in the system is the part that you don't see. There is always much more we need to know about and address in a situation before we "jump to conclusions" and make a hasty and poor decision that leads to poor outcomes. For example, will anyone managing the system recognize Sally's pride when she admonished Barbara for "not having her RN"? Are we sure that we understand Barbara's true motivations when she acted as she did and told Sally to help the patient herself? Will anyone take the time to understand Barbara's patient's wants and needs?

Our Job Relations method in TWI gives us the skill we need to follow the principle of *Respect Every Individual*, what Toyota likes to call Respect for People. Let's look at how Sally's manager used her JR skill to come to a good resolution to this problem. First, before she took any action on Sally's report, she considered what her objective was in handling the problem that came to her. She wanted to have Barbara, the PCA, willingly follow instructions from her supervising RN without disrupting patient care. But, at the same time, she wanted Sally, the RN, to manage the assisting workforce in a motivating way that created good teamwork across the floor. With that direction in clear view, she went about getting the facts in the situation.

Sally was an RN with 14 month's experience on the unit. She was hard working, ambitious, and had stated that she wanted to become a Charge Nurse because she had many ideas on how to improve the unit's function, including how to make assignments. Her working philosophy was that she was "in charge of her patient's care" and she delegated as she saw fit to meet the patient's needs. Sally primarily delegated to the PCA assigned to her patients but was willing to go to the nurse's desk or even other hallways to find someone else to fulfill the work if needed. Sally was direct and could be slightly abrupt in her communication style, but this was not viewed as disrespectful by the other staff. Most believed her approach and attitude were caused by her being Boston born and living in a southern culture.

Barbara had been on this unit for less than 3 months; this was her first PCA role in a hospital. She had worked before as a sitter/companion for homebound patients to have the self-scheduling flexibility she needed to care for her children while they were in preschool and elementary school. She had good evaluations from her preceptor (an experienced co-worker assigned to give personal instruction and guidance to new workers); she had received no complaints. In fact, she had been recognized once or twice during patient rounding as someone special.

The unit manager reviewed the facts:

- Sally – 14 months RN experience
  - Hard worker, ambitious
  - Direct and abrupt
  - Feels she is "in charge"
- Barbara – less than 90 days
  - Still within probation period
  - Previous experience w/homebound patients
  - Good evaluation from preceptor
  - No other complaints
- Patient needed help going to bathroom
- Did not answer phone twice
- Refused order to stop bathing patient
- Talked back
- RN angry
- Barbara stated: had been trying to find solution

Weighing these facts carefully, fitting them together, looking for gaps and contradictions, and relating them to each other to find cause-and-effect relationships, she could come up with various possible paths of action. Moreover, the unit manager could get a feel for the personal friction between the two employees, Sally's more rigid approach to "being the boss" versus Barbara's history of working more independently on her own schedule. These personality traits are not readily seen when you look only at the surface issues. Most tellingly, there were no signs that Barbara had work issues at all; she had even been praised by the patients, so the manager was cautious about a rush to judgment. She considered the following possible actions:

- Reprimand Barbara for insubordination
- Discuss and set priorities with group (e.g., going to bathroom vs. bathing)
- Review PCA job description with Barbara
- Coach Sally on leadership styles and skill

In deciding which actions to take from this list of possible actions, the unit manager considered that *Reprimanding Barbara* would not get her to her objective of having Barbara "willingly follow instructions" and having Sally "manage in a motivating way that created good team work." There was obviously a big "gap" in the facts between Barbara's refusal to follow an order and her history of no complaints. There was also a "contradiction" between her refusal to answer her phone and her spotless record of excellent patient care. If anything, a reprimand would demotivate Barbara, who was obviously trying to do her best for the patient. On the other hand, a reprimand, if not outright dismissal, was just what Sally was recommending in her report, and Sally would view this action in a very positive way. Nevertheless, the unit manager thought this action would negatively affect overall patient care since Barbara was doing a good job, and killing her enthusiasm would be a loss to the whole team. In this way, the unit manager weighed the plusses and minuses and came to the decision not to take this action.

The next possible action of *Discuss and set priorities with group* could, the manager thought, get her to her objective. With mutual agreement across the team, she could help foster better team work while having Barbara willingly follow the guidelines, even if that meant interrupting a bath to help another patient go to the bathroom. This would have a positive effect on the group as well, she thought, and improve patient care, though Sally might remain bitter about having her authority questioned. That is where the next two possible actions could help. By *Coach(ing) Sally on leadership styles and skill*, she could help Sally better understand and practice *Respect Every Individual*, one of the hospital's guiding principles, and develop a more effective approach to dealing with people. And by *Review(ing) PCA job description with Barbara*, she could help Barbara better understand that her role on a hospital team, where coordination of effort is critical, is different from working on your own and making decisions for yourself as she used to do in home patient care.

By carefully working through the problem using the Job Relations problem solving steps, the unit manager was able to take action that kept Barbara motivated and on the job while taking some forward steps in helping Sally become the manager she aspired to be. You can clearly see how this situation could quickly and easily have gone bad had the manager simply reacted to the emotion of the moment when there was conflict between the two employees. Resolving these situations, and managing the personal relationships that exist, largely unseen, until they "blow up" in your face, is the skill of leadership following the principle of *Respect Every Individual*.

As it turned out, the unit manager was able to get more insight when she was performing her patient rounds the next day and fill in the gaps in this case. The patient in room 9 expressed her desire to recognize Barbara for her compassion and kindness, saying Barbara behaved quite professionally when the nurse came charging into the room. It was her first day after surgery and she had asked Barbara to help her bathe before her family arrived to visit. The patient gratefully explained that Barbara had just refreshed the warm water and that she had asked Barbara not to stop to answer the phone so it wouldn't cool off. "I asked her for a little extra soaking – so she was delayed a bit," she said. The patient went on to say that the nurse was not very nice and never even acknowledged her or let her give her opinion. The nurse had actually told Barbara to stop the bathing and go to another room and help someone else – "I mean, really!!!" She had heard the nurse yelling at Barbara just outside her door and apologized for any trouble she may have caused by delaying her.

Considering that patient experience, or customer service, should always be at the top of our priorities, the unit manager was able to come to a good decision that worked to the best advantage of Barbara, Sally, and the hospital's patients.

Leading Is a Skill to Be Learned

We noted earlier in the book that TWI and Kata could be learned through practice and repetition. In every industry, whether manufacturing, health-care, service, or government, people get promoted because they are perceived as being good in a specific discipline, like being good nurses, operators, engineers, salesmen, etc. When they get promoted into leadership positions, the assumption is made, not always correctly, that they will also be good leaders, supervisors, managers, coaches, etc. The old adage in manufacturing plants, when a good operator is promoted to be the boss, is that "I just lost my best worker and got my worst supervisor."

A common misconception is that being a good leader is innate: You have it, or you don't. But we've learned, at least as far back as WWII with the Job Relations program, that leadership is a skill, like swimming or riding a bicycle, that can be developed through practice. What we've also learned is that just taking the 10-hour TWI-JR class is not enough to embed the method in the culture. As with any skill, it must be followed up on with good coaching and guidance (more on this in Chapter 5). When LEGO was standardizing Job Relations world-wide in their daily management culture, they pioneered an 8-week follow-up program in which newly trained leaders would meet once a week to review the method using current problems they were facing that week. What they found, and what we are continuing to find in numerous other implementations, is that leaders, while they get much out of the JR class, enjoy the "live" follow-up sessions much more for the practical application of the method in real time. Practice is where the method becomes "hard wired."

We are continually experimenting with ways to teach and embed the JR leadership skill, for example, following the LEGO model with weekly "lunch & learn" meetings to review cases like this one with Barbara. We write industry-specific case studies, taken from actual real-life examples, to give leaders practice dealing with defined situations using the JR method. We have developed practice guides to better utilize the Foundations for Good Relations that come with the JR practice (see next section: Application of Foundations for Good Relations). We do this for the same reason professional baseball players do batting practice before every game and professional golfers warm up at the driving range before every tournament. Even if you are a star athlete, you need to practice. Leadership is a skill that can be learned through practice.

Application of Foundations for Good Relations

In the traditional command-and-control management environment, a theme we continue to come back to again and again, management feels, or perhaps a better verb is "fears," that chaos will ensue if we, management, don't maintain strict control at all times. The insinuation here is that only management has the capability of keeping the ship afloat and preventing it from sinking. This shows a lack of respect for people and their motives. If we don't believe that they possess good intentions for the organization then we'll never trust them, regardless of their innate abilities, to make decisions and take actions on their own. We will always have to tell them what to do.

What about discipline? We must have some rules centered around basic standards of conduct to prevent unwanted behaviors like insubordination, violence, harassment, and major safety incidents. When we have "no tolerance" situations, and someone engages in violence, harassment, or even insubordination, we must let the person go because, at the end of the day, it is our duty to protect the integrity of the working environment and the business itself. However, we believe that, while necessary, this is nevertheless a failure of leadership because we did not get into the problem early and handle it while it was still small and easily resolved. The problem did not begin when the person committed the unforgiveable sin; it began as a small grievance or complaint that grew over time. When people are unhappy with their circumstances, they find ways of letting us know. If we brush them off or think, "They'll get over it," if we fail to listen and hear them out, their only recourse is to "turn up the volume" with poor attitude and bad behavior.

One of the core lessons of Job Relations is to get into problems while they are small and there are many good options still available, besides firing the person, to resolve the issue. In healthcare, with its perennial nursing shortages, as in all industries where skilled workers are hard to come by and take time to develop, we must fight for our people and do our best to help them stay on the job doing the good work they are capable of doing. The greatest respect we can pay people is to listen to their opinions and feelings and to empathize with their unique situations and treat them as individuals. When we work with them to resolve their problems, we do both them and our organizations a great service.

The Job Relations method, in addition to the 4-step method for solving people problems, gives us four Foundations for Good Relations that go directly to the core of the principle, *Respect Every Individual.* When these foundations are used regularly, they build and maintain strong relationships based on trust between people from all corners of the enterprise. When we *let each worker know how he or she is doing*, we give people regular feedback and allow them to be aware of needed adjustments in their behavior to stay on the path of growth and success. By setting clear expectations and pointing out ways to meet those expectations, we provide the support they need to do well. People are always looking for leadership and guidance; when they don't get it, they lose motivation or look elsewhere.

The single largest point of dissatisfaction in employees, and the reason they quit their jobs or are not engaged in their work, is they feel their efforts and contributions are not appreciated. This view is backed up by strong evidence from nationwide surveys going back many decades. The foundation here is to *give credit when due*, even simple words of thanks and appreciation when they are due, not months later buried in a blanket performance review. Every person wants to be appreciated, especially those who are exceptionally reliable whom we overlook because they work diligently but quietly, not seeking the spotlight.

Perhaps the next biggest source of frustration and anger people have with their employers is having change sprung upon them without any chance to have a say in the matter. We must *tell people in advance about changes that will affect them* so they can understand why the change is necessary and prepare appropriately. People oftentimes say, "It's not *what* they did, it's *how* they did it!" They didn't like what happened, but they are angry about the hurtful and harmful way it was done. As good leaders, we must work with our people to accept change, walking with them and guiding them through the emotions of adjusting to a new situation (see box: Working with People to Accept Change).

WORKING WITH PEOPLE TO ACCEPT CHANGE

Change is something that every organization must get used to. When people resist change, as they always do, leaders must have skill in helping them navigate the change and accept that the new way is replacing the old. We must *work with them to accept the change*, walking with them through the emotions human beings go through when dealing with loss. It is not unlike losing a loved one and going through the five stages of grief identified by researcher Elizabeth Kübler-Ross in her 1969 book, *On Death and Dying*: denial, anger, bargaining, depression, and acceptance. Change means having to let go of something we hold dear, the habits and routines that make up our daily life, and defined emotions come with that change.

When Patrick was explaining this to a new group of Job Relations trainers, one woman from Intel exclaimed, "That is just what happened in our plant in Costa Rica when management announced a change in promotion policy!" She went on to explain that, when the plant supervisors first heard about the new policy, they were in *denial* saying, "They will never do that; it will never happen." When it became clear that, in fact, this was going to be a change, she said they got *angry*, declaring they would quit if the new policy were enacted. They did not quit when the policy came on line but began to *bargain* with management, saying they would accept the new policy, but only with certain changes. When those changes were not made, they became *depressed*, claiming they would only do what they were told, "and nothing more!" Over time, though, once they recognized the resolve of the plant to enforce the policy, they came to *accept* it, and their work attitude returned to normal.

It is important to recognize that these emotions are normal and part of human nature. They should not reflect poorly on the people struggling with change; skillful leaders will recognize them and do a little "hand-holding," letting people "blow off steam," "walking with them through the fire" among other things, knowing that they will come out all right on the other side. Helping people adapt to change is one of the most important skills of a good leader. As Stephen Covey taught, "We do not give in, but we also do not give up." We respect our people enough to believe in them as we *work with them to accept change.*

The fourth foundation is to make *best use of each person's ability*; here, we pay respect to people by taking care not to hold them back simply to get our own job done. It is typical for a supervisor to want a good worker to keep doing the same job indefinitely, regardless of that person's ambitions and needs, so as not to interrupt the overall balance. Then the supervisor is shocked and dismayed when, one day, the worker has had enough and leaves for a better position, probably at a rival company. The only way for that worker to get ahead was to leave. Could a better position have been found in the original organization? Did the boss selfishly try to protect his or her own "turf" while ignoring the benefits the worker could have provided to the whole enterprise?

We have found, from many, many decades of teaching Job Relations and hearing countless examples of people problems in companies all over the world, that most, if not *all*, problems that relate to people in the workplace have their genesis in some failure by leadership to apply one or more of these foundations. When we fail to respect people in these four ways, we plant seeds of discontent that will fester, grow, and one day come back to be a significant problem that drags down the organization, often in very significant ways. When we fail to give workers feedback on a task and then blame them later for the failure, they may never forgive us. When people do something of real worth and we fail to show appreciation or say a word of thanks, they can hold a grudge for years to come. When we make a change, "stab them in the back," and "turn their lives upside down" by not letting them know ahead of time, they quickly forget the change that was made but forever remember the disruptive way it was done. When we prevent them from growing into and expressing the full breadth of their abilities, we can kill their motivation and simply invite them to take those good abilities elsewhere.

What we see with these foundations, and with the Job Relations problem-solving method overall, is that *Respect Every Individual* is not an abstract concept that we simply pay lip service. It is a skill that we can, and must, apply regularly. It is something that can be learned. Progressive organizations like LEGO standardize this aspect of their management system so that all employees, regardless of where they work, are consistently treated with respect.

One More (Manufacturing) Example

There are countless examples, like the Barbara Problem we looked at earlier, of how Job Relations has helped resolve people issues in a positive way. Dave Heim of Boeing in Seattle became a JR trainer with the intent to change the culture in his 5,000 employee division under his philosophy that, "Everyone should have a good boss." Dave himself tells his groups and conferences, "I wonder how many good people I have let go over the years, who could have continued making a contribution to the Boeing Company had I had this program?" This next example shows how JR helped a young supervisor keep a good employee on the job when the typical route would have been to fire the person. It is a bit of an old story, one from a small manufacturing workshop in Ohio, and one we used in another TWI book, *Implementing TWI: Creating and Managing a Skills-Based Culture*. A real incident brought into a JR class, it clearly demonstrates how the method delivers on respecting every individual and bears repeating.

A new supervisor had a person under his charge who had been a quiet but diligent worker at the company for many, many years. There had never been any problems to speak of with this person. Then, sometime in 2004, the worker became argumentative and difficult to work with for everyone in the factory. Since this was a small job shop, good communication and cooperation between the workers was key in processing small order sizes with a large variety of units. The young supervisor warned the worker about his behavior, that it was adversely affecting both the work environment and the output. The worker became angry at this admonishment, and his behavior got even worse. The supervisor tried again to talk with the person, imploring him to set a better example for the others, but it did no good.

In situations like this, as we pointed out in the last section, when employees' behavior deteriorates and they commit some "unforgiveable sin," such as refusing an order or threatening another employee, the typical result is that they are eventually terminated. Supervisors may even justify the action taken by saying that, in fact, the person "fired himself" with his unacceptable behavior. Unfortunately, and this is another common trait to these sad stories, the fired person is almost always a good worker, maybe one of the best in the department, and a replacement now has to be found and trained – a difficult and expensive process that does not always bring a better, or even equal, person to the one let go.

In this particular case, though, the young supervisor applied the JR method he was learning at the time. He listened to the person's "opinions and feelings" in order to get the whole story. He made a big effort, in spite of the hostility received from the disgruntled worker, to find the true cause of the bad behavior. It turned out the man was a Vietnam War veteran and was angry upon seeing the hero's welcome soldiers returning from the war in Iraq were receiving. "When we got back from 'Nam," he said bitterly, "we didn't get no parade." He explained how it was difficult to talk to anyone about these old wounds, especially to a young person like the supervisor who had not lived through that era.

Now that the problem was better understood, the supervisor could think of possible actions that could be taken to get to heart of the issue. This part of the JR method is the most critical; it recognizes that people are different – they are all individuals – and that no one action can apply to everyone because the cause of their behavior will never be the same. We can pay no greater respect than to treat people as the individuals they are. Without acting on the true cause of their behavior, we'll never come to a satisfactory solution. Veteran's Day came up shortly thereafter, and it was a holiday for the company. On that day, the supervisor called the man at home and, while saying he didn't want to bother him on his day off, told him he was thinking about him and thanked him for the service he had given to his country.

The action this supervisor took didn't cost him, or his company, a single dime. At the same time, it wasn't an easy thing for this young man to pick up the phone and express his sentiments after all the hard feelings between the two of them. He had to swallow some pride and admit to misunderstanding initially the employee's predicament. His action was effective, though, as the person's behavior returned to normal, and no adverse actions were taken against the employee. This example shows the power and simple genius of the TWI-JR method, and it demonstrates how the TWI methodologies are engrained with that human element that helps us deliver on our principle of respecting every individual.

Conclusion – Respect Must Be Given at All Levels

We like to say that Job Relations "operationalizes" the Lean pillar of Respect for People because it provides us with a specific method to practice and follow, rather than just giving platitudes and good feelings. There are many programs out there, and some very good ones dealing with managing people; they run the gamut from how to deal with problem employees to motivational programs that "pump up" enthusiasm and get people excited about the work at hand. Respect for people, if it is a skill to be learned and applied, must not be a "trick" or a "manipulation" of people, who in the long run, will figure this out. The effort will backfire on you. Manipulating people is the ultimate form of disrespect.

We hope that the content covered in this book appeals to more than just CEOs and executives. Great leadership can happen at every level of any organization, and we believe that it is rooted in respecting all people, developing trust, and leading with humility. Leaders at all levels of an organization can experience fatigue due to dictates from upper management. Unfortunately, some completely disengage from their most valuable asset – their people. Respect can be as simple as seeking input from front-line employees about where their frustrations or pain points are located. Alleviating some of those pain points can quickly build buy-in. Moreover, when you consistently apply the Foundations for Good Relations, you build strong relations that, in turn, lay the foundation for engagement and continuous improvement.

Consistently being respectful will build trust! Trust is key for creating a culture of improvement and operational excellence. Your team (it doesn't matter how large or how small it is) must first trust you if they are to follow you and engage in accomplishing the goals and objectives you set. Engagement is key to developing a sustainable culture, and every employee in the organization has something valuable to add to that development, but they will test you to see if you are truly sincere. When you are tested, how will you respond?

Chapter 4

How We Manage Ourselves

Whether through educational degrees or years of experience, some people who are given the responsibility to manage people mistakenly begin to think that their ideas are somehow better, that they have a better understanding of how a process should work, that front-line employees can't act properly without the commands of those in authority. These people hold the ill-informed view that their employees do not have the ability to come up with the needed solutions to their problems. They may even see it as their job to change people in a way that fits their views of how the work should run. These managers try to accomplish this change in a variety of ways, the worst of which, as we pointed out in the last chapter, being manipulation.

We have learned, from Stephen Covey and others, that the only person you can change is yourself. The change you affect in yourself will set a powerful example and lead, perhaps, others to follow your good example and make the change in themselves. That is why true leaders inspire others, not manipulate them. The worst thing you can tell someone is, "Do as I say, not as I do."

Lead with Humility

We make the point in TWI Job Relations, which teaches skill in leading, that a leader is a person who has followers. If no one is following you, then you are not leading. In that case, a "boss" is not necessarily a "leader." You may call yourself a leader and think of yourself as one, but you really are a "pusher." You push people to do things and use your positional authority to force them to do it. "To follow," on the other hand, has the connotation of "free will" in that the follower does so with volition and choice. To lead, then, means that you must inspire people to follow the path you wish to take them down.

TWI's Job Instruction component follows this same principle as well: "If the worker hasn't learned, the instructor hasn't taught." While the JI 4-Step Method gives us the skill (the how) to perform instruction well, this mantra gives us the principle (the why), which dictates the consequences of our action. Here the responsibility is on the instructor to skillfully teach the learner to perform the task with respect, valuing the worker's ability to learn the job. When we break down a job in preparation for instruction, looking for the "key points" that represent the real skill of the job, we also show respect for our skilled employees by listening to them to get their "tricks and knacks" for that job and using them when teaching it to others. In this way, we capture the true value of our organization, the hands-on experience of our veteran employees who are now able to pass on this know-how to the rest of the organization.

Finally, TWI's Job Methods improvement plan, as it was written and delivered in the 1940s, stresses that "operators have good ideas too; often just as many as we have – sometimes more!" This clearly teaches supervisors to follow the principle of *Respect Every Individual*, as we discussed in the last chapter, but what it, and all three TWI programs, demonstrates is an approach of humility in which leaders admit that the people closest to the process actually know more about it than they do. Most business cultures are based on the expectation that leadership and management are the experts and employees have been conditioned to defer to their judgment and decisions. Humility is needed if we want to move decision making to lower levels of the organization, closer to where the work actually gets done.

The paradox of strong leadership is that when you have been promoted to a "higher" position in an organization, you are called upon to act not with boastfulness but with humility, to be a good steward of the organization, its people, and its goals. Just when you thought you could celebrate your own ascension, you are called upon to show deference and respect for those who are to follow you, and this can be a lonely place for those not prepared. Lau Tzu, the ancient Chinese philosopher, gave us this piece of wisdom: *When the best leader's work is done, they will say, "We did it ourselves."* Bobby Knight, the popular and highly successful coach of the Indiana University basketball team from 1971 to 2000, is reported to have said, "When we won it was *their* victory, when we lost it was *my* failure."

Lead with Humility, the other guiding principle that is foundational to our ability to succeed in the People dimension of our Purpose – People – Process model (see Figure 1.1), means that we invest ourselves in the development of those we want to follow us while acknowledging our own limitations and weaknesses. This takes courage, but it allows us to delegate authority when appropriate instead of trying to prove ourselves by making every decision on our own, as if we had the best answer to every problem. The foundation of humility must first be firmly planted if we want the Process to succeed. We make a mistake in thinking that "the boss" is supposed to know everything and tell people what to do. The true leader guides his or her people to find the answers on their own, thus developing their abilities and gaining trust and cooperation.

In this respect, *Lead with Humility* really becomes the prerequisite to *Respect Every Individual*. The two principles are tied inextricably. Being able to authentically respect every individual comes from a place of true humility.

Peter Block, who introduced the business world to the word *empowerment* in his 1987 classic, *The Empowered Manager*, expanded on the principle of humility in his book on "servant leadership," which he called *Stewardship: Choosing Service over Self-Interest*. According to Block, "Stewardship is founded on the belief that others have the knowledge and the answers within themselves."[1] Block described how corporate leaders, with the best of intentions, continue to justify a command-and-control approach even as they profess a desire to serve the people of their organizations:

> There is something in the way leaders define themselves that inevitably becomes self-congratulatory and over-controlling. We expect leaders to choose service over self-interest, but it seems the choice is rarely made. Successful leaders begin to believe that a key task is to recreate themselves down through the organization. To make their beliefs and actions reproducible. They begin to wonder, "How do I instill in others the same vision and behaviors that have worked for me?" At the moment, this question may seem to the

---

[1] Peter Block, *Stewardship: Choosing Service over Self-Interest* (San Francisco, CA: Berrett-Koehler Publishers, Inc., 1993).

leader like a sincere desire to be of service, but to an observer, it has the stamp of self-interest.[2]

Trying to recreate yourself in others is not the mark of humility. Given the typical high turnover in management, with each new leader trying to create his or her own style, it is no wonder that employees are disengaged in the improvement process as they bounce from one philosophy and program to another. While they wait for this next greatest initiative to pass, as all the others have before it, they simply go about their business as they have always done and perform the work, as they have always done, regardless of who is in charge. Block postulated that, in the bigger scheme of life, we only get true power when the people we "lead" give it to us. It takes a humble person to realize that:

POWER IS GRANTED FROM THOSE BELOW

The community creates the opportunity for a person to be in a position of power. Power is bestowed upon us by those we "lead." We do not claim power, it is not passed on to us by others in power, we have no inherent right to power, whether by birthright, talent, or even achievement. If we serve those who put us in our position, then in an organization the recipients of our service and trusteeship are the core workers. They are the community, and they are the ones we become accountable to. We may be appointed by a board, or an executive, but they are given their authority as much by the people doing the work as by any other set of owners.[3]

Example of Servant Leadership

In 1987, Patrick was working for the Sanyo Electric Co. He was transferred from his training position in Japan to a new plant in Indiana that made compact discs (CD), a new technology at the time. Here is the story of a Japanese executive, Mr. Higuchi, who was the VP of production and showed great courage and humility in developing his staff and teaching them

---

[2] Ibid.
[3] Ibid.

how to run a new plant. While Higuchi was an exceptional leader in his own right who helped lead Sanyo's entry into the industry in Japan before he was assigned to the new United States plant, his approach to human development is typical of the philosophy and style used in Japan, where humility and respect for people are a deeply rooted part of the culture.

Sanyo had been one of the pioneers in developing the manufacturing technology for CDs, and had been exporting CDs to United States-based music companies for several years since their introduction in 1982. But the Indiana plant was a late comer and struggled mightily early on to get orders against stiff competition from rivals SONY and JVC, who already had well established and large facilities in the United States. Manufacturing prices were dropping, and worst of all, some of the major music companies had opened CD factories of their own. The Japanese had not anticipated this and had assumed that no American company would learn to replicate the complex processes of their technology, at least in the near term. There were real fears within Sanyo that the plant would not survive.

The only competitive edge the new plant had was accepting orders that other plants could not handle, in particular, those with difficult delivery dates. The Japanese CD manufacturers were used to long lead times from their exporting days and stubbornly held firm to those standards, but the biggest strategic advantage in the music business was time to market. As one music executive put it, "Selling music is like selling fruits and vegetables; if you don't get it out while it's fresh you can't even give it away!" Since the recording artists were typically late getting the finished tapes out of the studio, the manufacturing plants were always pressured to speed up product delivery.

With their backs to the walls, Patrick and the local production team were dedicated to seeing the new plant succeed and made a commitment that they would *never* be late on shipping an order. It was one thing under their control that could keep them competitive. Located in the Midwest, in the heart of car country, many of the young managers and supervisors had grown up seeing their parents lose their jobs as plants closed and moved down south or overseas. They did not want to suffer the same fate in this new industry that had come to their small city of Richmond, Indiana. But they were new and had lots to learn. As is typical for a Japanese company opening a new facility, they hired mostly younger people who were not necessarily "old hands" in the industry but had a good work ethic and were willing to learn. Patrick was 29 at the time, and he was one of the "old guys."

Their first major order came in from Motown and consisted of around ten titles for several thousand copies each. These were reissues of older albums or compilations of music from Motown's hey-day in the 1960s. It was a good start for a brand-new production plant. Patrick's job was to make and monitor the production schedule; he was in constant contact with the sales people and the customers themselves who liked to call the plant directly with their complaints and demands. The shipping date for this first order was a Friday; on Thursday morning, the final process supervisor came to Patrick with some bad news. He said, "We're not going to make it."

"What do you mean we're not going to make it!" Patrick exclaimed.

"We're not going to make it," the supervisor repeated.

"But we said we would *never* be late on an order," Patrick reminded him. The supervisor, with a long face, simply shrugged.

Patrick gathered the whole production team and went to see Mr. Higuchi. They told him they were not going to be able to ship the order the next day. Always a soft-spoken person, Mr. Higuchi said somewhat quietly, "I know."

"What do you mean you know?!" the team asked puzzled.

"I knew on Monday you weren't going to make it," Higuchi told them.

"What?! Why didn't you say anything?"

"I was just wondering when you would figure it out," he said with the slightest hint of a grin. The supervisors were not a little confused about why their boss had let them get caught in such a bind. Surely, they were thinking, he cared as much as they did about shipping the order on time.

"So, what should we do?" the supervisors asked.

"Oh, you want my opinion?" Higuchi asked.

"Yes, tell us what we need to do!" they implored.

"Let me just confirm," Higuchi continued with some persistence, "You want *me* to tell *you* what to do."

"Yes, we do!"

"OK," Higuchi said, "I just wanted to be sure we were clear on that."

Before giving his recommendations, he wanted to ensure that the local staff knew that they owned the final actions. What Higuchi had done, with his courage, discipline, and patience in waiting for the supervisors to discover their true standing on their own, without being told, was to create an environment in which his staff was open to guidance and willing to take it on their own volition. A leader is a person with followers, and here the wise Japanese production VP was able to motivate his staff to following his guidance.

Mr. Higuchi's next exchange was subtle but quite memorable and displayed his true humility and respect for the young green-behind-the-ears

Americans. He explained how when he and his team in Japan first started making CDs several years earlier, they too had experienced some of the same problems and made similar mistakes. It was an acknowledgement that he and the Japanese were no "better" than their new American colleagues, as he offered to make some suggestions as to what they had done in Japan to overcome the same difficulties. He did not insist in any way that this is what they could, or should, do to resolve the problem.

Higuchi explained how, if they wanted to keep the delivery deadline, they would have to work on Saturday to complete the production and get a special truck to pick up and deliver the product by Monday morning. They still had time. Fortunately for the plant, the company that manufactured most of the printed materials for the music industry was located in Indianapolis, just an hour down the road from Richmond, and they operated their own trucking company to haul product directly to music industry plants and distribution centers across the country. The trucking company was willing and able to pick up the shipment and take it directly to the customer's warehouse in Gloversville, NY. The production team was able to put together a crew for the overtime work, but as it turned out, they were still unable to finish after a full day of production on Saturday. So a small crew of final inspectors and packers came in Sunday morning to complete the order. It was picked up late Sunday afternoon and delivered Monday morning. (Higuchi later confided to Patrick that, in Japan, the workers would never have come out on a Sunday to work.)

That is not the end of the story. In the weeks and months that followed, because the supervisors were no longer afraid of taking their problems to their boss, they found failures and other difficulties and went to him for advice. His initial response was always the same, "I know." It seemed that he knew everything about every corner of the plant. Sometimes, though, in a very rare moment, one of the supervisors would report a problem that Higuchi didn't know about.

"Oh, really. I didn't know that," a puzzled Higuchi would admit.

"Gotcha!" the gleeful supervisor would shout out, fist pumping in the air, and then run through the plant telling everyone how he had "found a problem that Mr. Higuchi didn't know about." It became a running contest to "find the problem that Mr. Higuchi doesn't know about," a contest with no prizes or rewards, just the satisfaction of seeing who could beat Higuchi at his best and find a problem he was unaware of. The end result was that the staff became practiced, and then skilled, at seeking out and finding problems while they were still in the early stages and could be solved quickly before they caused greater damage. As we have already pointed out, this is what the Japanese like to call *mondai ishiki*, or problem consciousness, and Higuchi succeeded at accomplishing his critical role of developing his staff so they could run the plant on their own without being told what to do.

While there were some other big pieces to the story, because of Higuchi's great efforts at developing the capability of his new staff to meet the challenges they faced in a difficult start up environment, the plant succeeded in becoming both competitive and profitable and, over the first five years, while Patrick played daily jujitsu with the production schedule, they would never once be late on a promised delivery date. In fact, the plant became so good at meeting the most difficult demands that it became the go-to site for production when music companies, for example, needed to get a title "on sale" to meet a deadline for Grammy nominations or when a new single had been promoted but the recording tape didn't come out of the studio until the weekend before its debut date. The record companies rewarded them for their efforts with good orders that filled up the plant to capacity on a regular basis.

A Lesson in Humility – Nick Saban's Loss in the 2019 Championship Game

As we were finishing up the final draft of this manuscript, having written so much on Nick Saban's coaching style and using it as an example for what we think is effective leadership, we anxiously anticipated the national championship game on January 7, 2019, between Alabama and Clemson. We watched in horror as Clemson routed the Crimson Tide 44–16 in the worst loss ever for a Saban-led Alabama team, which had never lost any game by more than 14 points. As *Sports Illustrated* reported, "Alabama was too sloppy, too undisciplined and made too many mistakes. All of which were unfamiliar territory for a group of seniors that had only lost three games in four years before this one."

One big lesson we can draw from this experience is that even the best of us is always only one game away from total defeat.[4] It would be easy to find blame for the loss in the many mistakes made or the uncharacteristic coaching calls, like a fake field goal that ended up in a two-yard loss. We

---

[4] We will speak much more on the topic of entropy and sustainment in the final chapter of the book.

could criticize the players for not following "the process" or simply say that the other's teams star players, who truly were super, were too much for us to beat. In spite of all past glory and countless accolades, the true leader must stand up and, with humility, accept responsibility for the outcome. "I think the responsibility for us not playing well really starts with me," Saban said after the loss.

It is instructive to see the response from Coach Saban as the team immediately began self-assessing where they had gone wrong and what needed to change. Coach Saban's greatest strength may be his ability to adapt and evolve his management system over the years, to adjust to changes in the game and continue to compete for championships as the head football coach for the Crimson Tide for an unprecedented decade and counting. For example, there have been changes to the look of his defense and an embrace of an RPO (Run/Pass Option) style offense, even after he was the loudest critic of this style of play. You also see Coach Saban bring in a myriad of coaches to learn and adapt to his systems. After this year's loss, at least five assistant coaches will change or be replaced, yet another adjustment to the management system of the greatest college football coach of all time.

Saban commented on how, many times, you learn more from a loss than a win. When Alabama lost to Clemson on a last-second play two years ago, Saban was quoted as saying, "Don't waste a failure." He got some negative press for that comment because his team was two seconds away from a national championship and he was calling it a failure. This is just how he looks at his job – any loss is a failure, no matter how many wins he has.

If you ask Saban to recall any specific game in his career, it's not the wins but the losses that he remembers. Each loss usually comes with self-evaluation and adaptation to things he wants to change about the program. This is very true with this year's loss. "I just have a feeling that I didn't do a very good job for our team, giving them the best opportunity to be successful," Saban proclaimed. "I always feel that way, even sometimes when we win, I think there's things we could do better or that I could have done better." True to form, Saban is always looking beyond the score, whether they win or lose, and never ceases asking, "How are we playing the game?"

Conclusion – People before Process

It is an overused adage that an organization's most important resource is its people. Perhaps another take on this would be to say that if the People dimension of the management system is not securely in place, the Processes never get us to the Purpose for our existence. In other words, a bad human environment will take down a good process any day. If the lubrication is missing from the gear train, the best designed machine in the world with the best quality parts will freeze up and break down. So it is with human relations.

Our focus on principles has shown us that we are in control of the consequences we get from our management systems because we can work on our own attitudes and approach to *Lead with Humility* which, in turn, creates capacity for us to *Respect Every Individual* under our charge. The image of a "servant leader" or, as we will define in the next chapter, a "shepherd," is a good one. How do you see yourself in front of your people? Do you have the humility to be in the service of those you lead? Whether you are a CEO or a front-line operator or staff person, you will be given the role of leader by those who choose to follow you, but only if they see you first as their humble servant, guiding them to a better place.

Now that we have laid out the "mindset" and prepared a strong and proper foundation of People, we will move forward to look at the dimension of Process in a management system in Part 3.

Executing Process

3

Chapter 5

How We See the Work

Many years ago, when Kaizen Events were gaining wide usage and Lean study and practice was spreading quickly throughout the manufacturing environment, a Japanese executive from Toyota was heard saying, "Kaizen is not an *event*, it is a *way of life*." In other words, while continuous improvement has lots of related practices and skills, it should not be thought of as an "activity" to be performed on a predefined scheduled, but rather a "philosophy" that permeates the very essence of a successful management system. Kaizen, in this view, is not something extra, added to the regular work we do each day; it is an integral part of that daily work. Unfortunately, new improvement tools and systems are often received as just being extra work for the department.

Following our guiding principle of *Seek Perfection*, how can we create a culture that continuously seeks perfection in everything it does? In our contemporary model of continuous improvement, organizations may rely on these kinds of scheduled events to make even small changes, so when people have an issue that needs to be addressed they think, "We'll take care of that during the next Kaizen Event." Moreover, since these events and programs are typically run by experts or staff dedicated to them, these same employees will tend to rely on those experts to come up with the improvement ideas, along with the implementation, even when they are invited to participate. In that case, the improvement work is not owned by the department itself, but by the experts and their improvement department. If they are left to take charge of the improvement process themselves, they may not have the needed skills and experience to effectively resolve the issue. They will certainly not have the ability to continue the kaizen effort until that improvement activity becomes a part of their daily work. In any case, both managers and employees typically leave any improvement work until "after we make the numbers" which, in reality, never comes.

If continuous improvement is truly to become "a way of life," it must be integrated into the management system so that its practice becomes a regular part of the system. Pascal Dennis, in his book *Getting the Right Things Done*, put it this way:

> Managerial work has two parts: routine work and improvement work. The formal organizational structure is good at the former, but not so good at the latter because improvement work requires cross functionality. Moreover, many managers believe their job has no relation to improvement and make no space for it in their daily work. Others would like to make space for improvement work but are overwhelmed by the crises of the day. Strategy deployment puts improvement work on the radar screen and keeps it there.[1]

This means that the components of the management system, the "gears," must both represent and facilitate the kaizen philosophy, the endless pursuit of perfection, so that the system itself embodies continuous improvement. We like to think of that as "working on the work" which can, as a rule of thumb, be conceptualized as the organization spending 80% of its time doing the work, while 20% of the organization's time is spent "working on the work" (see Figure 5.1). This rule takes into account everyone in the organization with, of course, those percentages changing depending on the individual's role. Some employees may spend a few minutes each day working on improvement while others might spend the bulk of their working day improving the system.

An Alternative to Command-and-Control

Throughout this book we have contrasted our thoughts on a more participative and integrated management system with the traditional Western

---

[1] Pascal Dennis, *Getting the Right Things Done* (Cambridge, MA: The Lean Enterprise Institute, Inc., 2006).

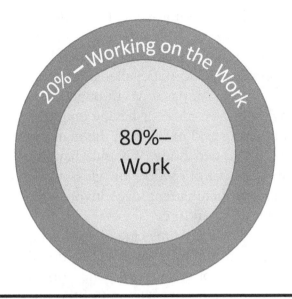

Figure 5.1   Work vs. "Working on the Work"

model of management, the command-and-control style where the "white-collar" *thinkers* of an organization come up with a plan of action to take against some problem or challenge while the "blue-collar" *doers* are charged with implementing that plan without any chance of giving their insights or opinions. In that model, management's job from that point forward is to hold the workers accountable for executing the fix, the concept being that, since the plan is "perfectly" (or at least "professionally") conceived, its failure can only be due to the lack of effort, skill, or motivation on the part of the laborers. Finding someone to blame for failure, however, is the mindset of a victim and is not productive.

Command-and-control managers are oftentimes looked down upon by Lean practitioners who frame them as "bad managers," but we should not rush to judgment. Many managers, as they profess loyalty to the concepts of workplace democracy, may not even recognize their own behaviors and style of managing and cannot imagine that they are, in fact, command-and-control managers. They are simply who they were taught to be, most likely following a pattern learned in the stable business environment in which they were brought up. In a more agile, competitive environment, when that pattern fails to succeed, the thinking and behavior continues.

It has been long argued and definitively proven that front-line workers, who have direct experience making and delivering the product or service, have the best ideas on how to improve it. This follows our guiding principle to *Assure Quality at the Source*. Yet many organizations, even as they diligently try to apply a more humanistic approach, including superficial Lean implementation models, do not challenge this core way of thinking about the need for control. They may go through the motions of, for example, collecting employee ideas or having employees participate in kaizen activities, but at the end of the day, the managers make the final decisions on anything that gets done. Without changing our core beliefs on how we see and think about our work, just glossing it over with "feel good" notions and programs for getting employee involvement only creates cynicism and distrust with the workforce.

Don't get us wrong. There are times in any leadership in which the person in charge has to take control. If the building is on fire, literally or figuratively, you do not have the luxury of getting everyone's opinions and feelings on evacuation. The command is given, "Get out of the building!" and everyone must comply. Employees at W. L. Gore, one of the very earliest and most enduring examples of an organization using participatory management and a matrix organization chart,[2] enforce the concept of "waterline," which means that individuals and teams can make decisions on their own as long as they are "above the waterline." In other words, if you punch a hole in the boat that is "above the waterline," the boat will not sink and we can always go back and repair the hole. But if the hole you make is "below the waterline" and failure could sink the boat (i.e., the company), then the team needs to consult with other associates to move forward.[3] As we can see, an effective management style is situationally dependent and not black and white.

Interestingly, the TWI founders in the United States tackled and successfully addressed these same challenges during WWII in the 1940s. What is more, when the TWI fundamentals went to Japan in the early 1950s, they provided critical groundwork for what evolved into standard Japanese business practice, best embodied in the Toyota Production System and the pattern of work at Toyota that Mike Rother found during his research on Toyota Kata. For example, the "mantra" of TWI Job Instruction is, "If the

---

[2] At W.L. Gore, no one has a boss, just a sponsor; team members are hired, evaluated, compensated, and fired by their peers. Employees are not "ordered" to do anything but make "commitments" to work on projects.

[3] From discussions with W.L. Gore associates. Also, see Gary Hamel's excellent article on W.L. Gore history and management style, "Innovation Democracy: W.L. Gore's Original Management Model." (www.managementexchange.com/story/innovation-democracy-wl-gores-original-management-model).

worker hasn't learned, the instructor hasn't taught." The TWI founders knew that if workers, whether in a factory, an office, or a hospital, could not execute their work properly, the fault lay with management for not teaching well; Toyota took this lesson to heart when it adopted the Job Instruction method, which is still used in all Toyota plants today. When we explain to Toyota veterans the history of TWI, they almost always tell us, many with disbelief and astonishment in their eyes, that they assumed this "mantra" was Japanese or unique to Toyota because it so embodies the philosophy of how Toyota manages its people.

In TWI's Job Methods Improvement program, also developed during WWII, we find the seeds of the kaizen philosophy, which is at the core of Lean practice as it was developed in Japan. In his groundbreaking research on TWI, which reintroduced these methods into the United States, Dr. Alan Robinson reported, "JM is often credited for its role in the development of *kaizen* ('continuous improvement') in Japan, now a distinctive part of the management style of that country."[4] In his subsequent work on idea management systems,[5] Robinson calls JM an "Idea Activator" because it creates skill in bringing out the creativity of front-line workers. In the original JM training manual from the 1940s, you find expressions like

- Work out your ideas with others.
- Operators have good ideas too; often just as many as we have – sometimes more!
- Put the new method to work – use it until a better way is developed.
- Remember there will always be a better way. Keep searching for further improvements.
- We can't afford to be too busy to find time to continually search for improvements.

These kinds of directives should sound very familiar to those trying to create a Continuous Improvement working environment, but as we can see from history, they are not new and, for that matter, they are not Japanese.

---

[4] Alan G. Robinson and Dean M. Schroeder, "Training, Continuous Improvement, and Human Relations: The U.S. TWI Programs and the Japanese Management Style," *California Management Review* (Winter 1993).

[5] Alan G. Robinson and Dean M. Schroeder, *The Idea-Driven Organization: Unlocking the Power in Bottom-Up Ideas* (San Francisco, CA: Berrett-Koehler Publishers, Inc., 2014).

These examples show that breaking away from a strict command-and-control system is not "new age psychology," but rather good common sense that works. It certainly made a big contribution to winning WWII as we saw from TWI's history in Chapter 1. What can we do differently, then, from what we are doing now? It has to do with how we see and think about the work.

Experimentation, Not Implementation

John Shook, senior advisor and executive chairman of the Lean Enterprise Institute, fondly tells the story of how Fujio Cho, former Chairman of Toyota who worked with Shook in different capacities over many years, always answered a question with another question. Even as Chairman, Cho maintained personable speaking relationships with all of Toyota's employees, even front-line workers, who regularly sought out his opinion on daily issues. However, he never gave them answers to their questions. Instead, he pointed them, through his return questions, in the right direction, allowing the questioners to find answers on their own. This is the way Japanese managers, at all levels of an organization, coach the development of their people, like we saw with Patrick's old boss, Mr. Higuchi, in Chapter 4. It also shows their ability to let people learn through experience, which means experimenting with their own ideas to see what works as well as what doesn't.

Patrick has fond memories of one Japanese manager at Sanyo Electric in Japan who always yelled out, in a strange combination of frustration and glee, "*Yarinaoshi!*," when one of the staff failed at a task or project. In Japanese, *yaru* means "to do" while *naosu* means "to fix," and the compound word means to "redo" or, in this case, "Try again!" What this manager did, as Kata students would learn decades later, was to allow his staff members to try on their own and even fail as they "experimented" their way forward to finding the solution to their dilemma. Compare this to the command-and-control environment pattern of telling them what to do and blaming them for any poor results. In a Japanese management system, the manager's role is to act as coach and teacher in the development of the people; John and Patrick look back on these experiences with such affection because they know the great opportunity they had as young men to learn and grow under these leaders.

It was no surprise for us, given this background, to find in the Kata methodology an emphasis on experimentation and the Plan-Do-Study-Act (PDSA) cycle (see Figure 5.2). Students of William Edwards Deming will

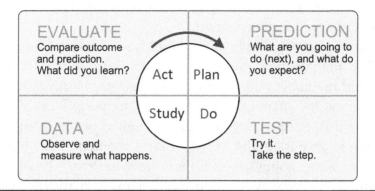

Figure 5.2   PDSA Cycle – Scientific Method

know that PDSA is a cycle that continues endlessly as we move closer to our goal of perfection, utilizing the scientific method of posing hypotheses and experimenting to test for validity; this methodology forms the basis of continuous improvement. It also allows us to follow our guiding principle of *Embrace Scientific Thinking*. Kata added a pattern we can practice with the goal of embedding this developmental coaching as a regular part of the culture. It takes practice, along with large doses of fortitude and patience, to break our previous patterns of command-and-control and allow our people to act on their own ideas, even if they fail along the way to success.

The key here is to move from an *implementation* mindset to an *experimentation* mindset where, as management, we no longer assume we have, or even need to have, all the answers ahead of time. As management, we set where we want to go and let our people navigate the unknown territory on how to get there. This new pattern recognizes that we must make it OK for people to fail, something that will come as a big surprise to those used to working under the old order. Think about it. Failure is one of our best teachers, so long as we fail safely. Just like good parents teaching babies to walk or young children to ride bicycles, managers must let workers fall down if they are ever to learn skills. If you continue holding onto their hands, or holding the seats while running alongside the bike, they will never be able to find their balance and move forward independently and confidently. In the same way, by teaching your employees to stand up by themselves, literally and figuratively, you are opening your organization to the wealth of knowledge, experience, creativity, and inspiration latently locked up in each employee, the finest aspects of the people you bring into your organization every day. These are the very things that are squelched and buried in a command-and-control environment.

This doesn't mean we simply allow employees to do whatever they want. That would be management malpractice. When introducing Job Relations to a 100+-year-old manufacturing company in Chicago, Patrick advocated front-line supervisors at the plant taking actions on the people problems they faced. Hearing this, the production manager yelled out in exasperation, "Are you just going to give them the keys?!" After a moment of thought, he answered, "No, we're going to teach them how to drive." If we want our people to take responsibility for their work, actively participate in finding solutions for their problems, and make improvements to their work, we must teach them skills to adequately do so. This is the essence of what TWI did during WWII and continues to do today. We must be diligent in following up and coaching to ensure workers find success in these efforts.

More details will be given on how to practice these system components in the next chapter, but how we see the work and think about the people doing that work is key to effectively running a management system. Have we set up and aligned our system in a way that people can fully engage in and practice the process? Have we developed human relations to the point at which mutual respect and trust allows the process to take place?

Example of TWI Job Methods Practice in Continuous Improvement

A front-line manager in charge of perioperative care at a large hospital was taking the Job Methods training class, two hours per day over a five-day period, when a big problem arose on Wednesday. Perioperative care is the treatment of a patient before and after surgery, and blood was drawn by a phlebotomist[6] from the lab on a patient who was getting ready for surgery. It was imperative that blood be drawn from the opposite, non-operative, side of the body so as not to jeopardize the ability to perform the surgery, but the phlebotomist mistakenly drew blood from the operative side. What made matters worse is that the same mistake had occurred just two weeks earlier, and the surgeon was frustrated and angry at these unnecessary delays.

---

[6] A specialist who draws and prepares blood for medical testing, transfusions, or donation.

When he heard about it, the manager's first inclination was to call up the lab manager and give her a piece of his mind. How could this have happened again?! Why didn't the lab tech follow the procedure of drawing blood from the arm that did *not* have the patient's arm band attached, the rule that prevented this mistake from happening? Obviously, the gears of the system here were slipping and grinding between the Operating Room and the Lab.

But Mike, the manager in charge, thought to himself, "I'm taking this JM class, so why don't I try and use it to see if I can make this better? What do I have to lose?"

Mike was able to use his new skills to question those details and come up with improvement ideas to prevent the mistake from being repeated (see Table 5.1). In the current method, the EMR (Electronic Medical Records) system automatically assigned the blood draw procedure as a "Lab Draw," rather than a "Nurse Draw," which meant that once the orders were entered into the system the lab was automatically scheduled to come to the surgery holding room to collect the blood before surgery. Following the JM method, Mike questioned why this was necessary; after talking with the nurses in the area, he learned that when the EMR system was put into place three years earlier the staff had been unsure as to how the new computer system would behave. To play it safe, they set it up as an automatic Lab Draw since the Lab staff specialists could better adapt to unusual or difficult circumstances

Table 5.1   Current Method JM Breakdown Sheet for "Date of Surgery Blood Draw"

Job Breakdown Sheet

PROCESS: Date of Surgery (DOS) Blood Draw — MADE BY: Mike T. — DATE: Aug. 16, 2016
OPERATIONS: ID check, blood draw, label specimen — DEPARTMENT: Peri-Op

	CURRENT METHOD DETAILS	Distance traveled in feet	REMARKS TIME/TOLERANCE/ REJECTS/SAFETY	WHY-WHAT	WHERE	WHEN	WHO	HOW	IDEAS Write them down, don't try to remember.	Eliminate	Combine	Rearrange	Simplify
1	Place arm band on patient (pt)		On non-operative side										
2	Release orders in EPIC		Include Bay #										
3	Lab receives orders		Automatic setting: Lab, not Nurse Draw	X					Find out why. Nurse can draw if able to print labels	X			
4	Print labels				X	X	X		Place label printer in holding area			X	
5	Lab tech walks to Pre-op	200 ft.		X					No, if nurse draws when starting IV	X			
6	Check white board at nurses' station			X					Same as #5	X			
7	Walk to holding area	50 ft.		X					Same as #5	X			
8	Verify pt's name & DOB		Looking at armband			X	X		Already done by nurse on entry to room		X		
9	Draw blood		From non-operative side			X	X	X	When nurse starts IV, no need to stick patient twice		X		X
10	Label specimens				X		X		Print in holding area			X	
11	Transport to lab	250 ft.						X	Use tube system				X
12	Run lab test												

created by the new system. As the EMR system had now been in place for several years, that was no longer a concern.

With this new insight, Mike had the idea to have the Perioperative nurses, who were directly preparing the patient for surgery, do the blood draw since they were already setting up an IV for the patient and knew very clearly which side of the patient's body to draw from. Even better, they could draw the blood samples directly from this IV port they had already inserted, so there would no longer be a need to "stick" the patient twice. The only problem was that they needed the labels to put on the sample tubes. One of the nurses came up with the idea of putting a printer in the holding area and having the labels printed right there instead of in the lab. "The printers are all connected to the EMR," she stated, "so what difference does it make where the labels are printed?" A pneumatic tube transport system was already in place, and samples could be sent directly to the lab using the canisters that already sent X-rays, patient results, drugs, and test results throughout the hospital. His proposed method greatly reduced the risk of error and eliminated a lot of travel time and effort by the phlebotomist who would no longer have to come to the surgery to collect the blood (see Table 5.2).

Mike was worried, though. Would the lab staff be offended by his proposal and resist the change thinking he was stepping on their turf? As it turned out, the lab supervisor was also attending the JM class that week; she heard Mike's presentation on his improvement proposal the next day and

Table 5.2 Proposed Method JM Breakdown Sheet for "Date of Surgery Blood Draw"

Job Breakdown Sheet

PROCESS: Date of Surgery (DOS) Blood Draw MADE BY: Mike T. DATE: Aug. 16, 2016
OPERATIONS: ID check, blood draw, label specimen DEPARTMENT: Peri-Op

	PROPOSED METHOD DETAILS	Distance traveled in feet	REMARKS TIME/TOLERANCE/ REJECTS/SAFETY
1	Place armband on patient		On non-operative arm
2	Release orders in EPIC		
3	Verify patient name & DOB	5-10 ft.	At bedside
4	Collect IV & blood draw supplies		
5	Start IV and draw blood		
6	Label/Collect at bedside		
7	Transport to lab through tube system	20 ft.	

was elated. "You mean," she said, "our techs no longer need to interrupt their daily rounds in the hospital to walk all the way over to the OR holding rooms for a surgery? That's great! When can we start?"

By utilizing the TWI Job Methods skill as one of the components of the management system, the Perioperative Manager was better able to "connect the dots" between his department and the Lab making the work they needed to coordinate more efficient and error free. Moreover, he was able to develop the improvement himself, with cooperation from his team, using his new-found JM skill without having to rely on "experts" or being told what to do by upper management. JM gave him the skill in developing a questioning mindset, and that is where his improvement ideas were born.

Focus on Process

In Chapter 1, we saw how Kata practice gave us a pattern to follow, at any level in the organization, for moving toward multiple target conditions that guide us to our challenge (see Figure 1.3), which is aligned to the greater goals, or *hoshins*, of the whole organization. In this way we gradually become more and more capable of "connecting the dots" from the very highest aspirations of the organization all the way down to the actions and activities at the front lines. Whether we are using the Kata routines or any other practices that drive us to our goals, the key, when we carry out these elements of the management system we have put in place, is to maintain focus on the process, not the immediate results. Alabama's football coach, Nick Saban, likes to call that the inner scoreboard where we keep track of "how we are *playing* the game," not simply who is *winning* the game. Are we sticking to our process and executing flawlessly? If so, then the outer scoreboard, that everyone else sees, will take care of itself.

In Chapter 2, we focused on how Kata practice helps facilitate alignment of the system components, but let's drill down a little deeper as we look at how we actually see and do the work. We see the work of the management system as *following a process*, much as Coach Saban insists on his players following "the system" meticulously and not show-boating or trying to win the game on your own as a "superstar," even if that play scores a touchdown. The Kata routines are meta-processes, they stay the same regardless of the circumstances. The *what* of the work will be different, but the *how* will always be the same. Our focus should be on the process, on *how* we do the work, regardless of the content of that work. If we follow, practice, and perfect the *how*, like the Kata improvement and coaching routines, then our thinking will be influenced by our evolving behavior and the fruits of those efforts. Remember, "It is easier to act your way into a new way of thinking, than to think your way into a new way of acting."

In the Kata coaching routine, the coach never tells or gives the learner the answers to the coaching questions about target condition and obstacles. These answers must come from the learner as must the answers to what to try next as you "experiment" your way forward, engaging the PDSA cycle, to overcome that obstacle. The "experiments" we run to test our hypotheses must come from the ingenuity and inspiration of those running them, the learners, if we are ever to have them learn and grow. At the same time, however, the process we go through in order to move toward our targets, and ultimately the big challenges faced by the whole organization, must be firmly enforced and executed.

Let's state that again: The role of management is to enforce the process, not to tell people what to do. Many managers like to call this empowerment but, as Stephen Covey taught us, empowerment does not mean abandonment. Empowering a person to take charge of a situation does not relieve us of our responsibility to coach and give support for that work. Our challenging role as management is to run the management system, which means teaching, coaching, and enforcing the process. We are fully engaged, at the *gemba*, every step of the way. Interestingly, whenever Alabama players are interviewed after a football game on what they did to win and how, they always answer in the same way, "It's part of the process." They sound like their coach, who follows the principles of *Seek Perfection* and *Focus on Process*.

Shepherding Groups and Their Role in Process

Another critical element of the management system, in helping change the culture and ensure leaders are "connecting the dots," is something we call the Shepherding Groups. These groups of leaders who already use elements of the management system are willing to assist other departments in their journeys by promulgating a way of thinking and practicing the system fundamentals until they become part of the daily culture. An old metaphor to management was "herding cats," and this image is quite appropriate for directing people to move in a unified manner and direction. Working for a Christian-based organization, we like the image of a shepherd leading the flock. You can also think of these teams in terms of steering committees, thought leaders, action teams, or process promotion groups.

The Shepherding Groups create and facilitate daily routines that link the various elements of the management system. The routines are, of course, the *how* of the process. The Shepherding Groups can be formed at all levels of the organization; their existence ebbs and flows as the focus of the organization and the individual departments changes. They typically consist of five to seven people who are experienced in the process, in our case exceptional Kata coaches, to steer the development of the Kata practice or, as our people call it, to "Kata the Kata." They utilize the Kata process in the shepherding work they are trying to instill in their target areas whether at a high level, like a CFO trying to cut overall business costs, or at a departmental level, like a warehouse manager trying to reduce spoilage.

The Shepherding Group starts by organizing Kata training with the people under their charge and then immediately get the Kata practice up and running, ensuring the desired pattern of practice. The goal in the first phase is to embed the practice into the area. Then the Shepherds help coaches "drive a wedge" of an hour into their busy working days, 15 minutes to coach, 30 minutes to conduct the experiment, and 15 minutes to reflect on the learning and update the storyboard. New Kata practitioners typically spend a long time at these activities, getting bogged down; the Shepherds help them stay on track so they don't give up. The Shepherds assist in setting reachable target conditions and ensure the coaches are working on obstacles that are actually connected to the target conditions. New practitioners often jump at the first issues they find in front of them, issues that are not necessarily "aligned" with the target condition. The Shepherds then guide coaches through the PDSA cycles, giving feedback on the number of cycles they complete, how long they take to complete them, and whether they are gravitating toward the challenge. Table 5.3 shows the Kata Dashboard used by the Shepherding Groups to keep track of the coaching teams they are supervising.

Kata training alone will not get people to "think their way into this behavior." As we've stated many times, just because you know something is good to do doesn't mean you will have the fortitude to continue doing it. By guiding them down the path to "act their way into a new way of thinking," the Shepherds help employees change the perception of their own work, which in turn changes the way they think about and do that work on a regular basis.

After an area becomes embedded in the practice, the Shepherding Group will back off a bit allowing the coaching teams to begin carrying on by themselves. Now that the Kata pattern is being followed, the Shepherds want

Table 5.3 Kata Dashboard

KATA Boards - 2019	Coaching Cycle Time	Learner	Coach	2nd Coach	Shepherd	Challenge	Aligned to which "Right(s)"?	Last Date board owner updated dashboard	Challenge Outcome Metric

Starting Outcome Metric (At the beginning of the Challenge)	Current Outcome Metric (At the end of the Target Condition)	Year to Date Outcome Metric	Trending Toward or Away from Challenge	Target Condition #	Last TC Theme	# PDSA cycles during last Target Condition	Last Attainment Fraction and Percentage	YTD Attainment Percentage

to ensure the teams are doing a good job of practicing the routines. The Shepherding Group will change its focus from driving the practice to checking the quality of the practice and ensuring the pattern and flow are smooth and routine. By quality, we mean they are checking the linkages between the elements of the storyboard, in particular, the "triangle" of target condition – obstacle – PDSA cycle (see Figure 5.3). Does the target condition move the team toward the challenge? Does the obstacle being worked on identify and describe a specific gap in the working patterns between the current and target conditions? Does the PDSA cycle address a specific obstacle? Notice, again, the Shepherds are *not* looking at the content of the improvements, the details of what is being done and how, but only the *process* the coaches are engaged in and how it is carried out.

In the third phase, the shepherds will introduce the concept of a "2nd Coach," which is the "coach's coach," who gives feedback and guidance to those running the Kata coaching cycles. Developing this additional skill allows the teams to begin managing themselves in the Kata practice, taking over this function from the Shepherding Groups. In the next two phases, the

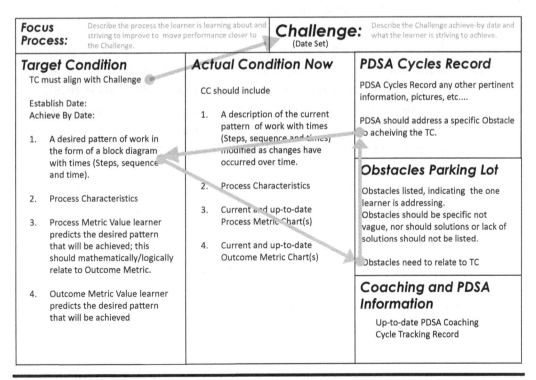

Figure 5.3   Kata Board "Triangle": Target Condition – Obstacle – PDSA

Shepherds move into the expansion phase where they start looking for additional areas or departments to begin new Kata projects. They do this with assessment practices in their current teams, beginning with a self-assessment and then a detailed assessment, by the Shepherds, of practitioner skills. This sets the Shepherds up to recognize the exceptional coaches and to create and run new initiatives using the advanced skills of these now experienced practitioners.

The five-phase Kata development cycle can be summed up as follows[7]:

Phase 1 – Pattern of Practice
Phase 2 – Quality of Practice
Phase 3 – Second Coach Development
Phase 4 – Self-Skill Assessment
Phase 5 – Shepherd Group Assessment of Practitioner Skill
Expansion to Other Areas and Departments

We have organized these phases on a month-by-month basis, but there is no set rule for how long each phase should run. The importance is to develop understanding and adoption in each phase to ensure that the leader and the department build routines that will continue.

In this way, the coaching Kata can be expanded, step-by-step, to all levels of the organization creating a standard process of how we play "catch ball" as an integral means to maintaining alignment of the management system.[8] A manager, for example, might be a coach to a supervisor who is running a Kata in her section on reducing defects in the final assembly area. At the same time, this same manager himself might be a learner being coached by his director on improving quality in the overall production process. This director herself might be a learner to an administrator running a Kata on improving customer service. Here, then, the higher-level management will set a target condition that will become the challenge for the next level below. With everyone at each level of the organization "speaking the same language" and following the same process, we create *keystone habits* in these meta-processes across the organization and build innate capability to keep the management system in alignment as we carry out the work up and down the organization. Figure 5.4 outlines this process.

---

[7] This model was developed and implemented with Beth Carrington and Brandon Brown, two experts on the Kata methodology.
[8] See Chapter 2 for a more detailed explanation of "catch ball" and its role in alignment.

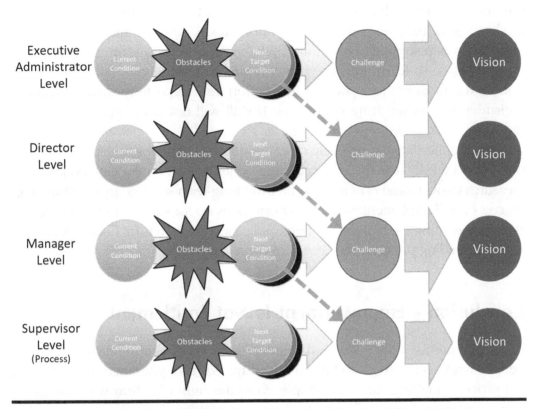

Figure 5.4 Kata Practice at 4 Levels: Executive Administrator, Director, Manager, Supervisor

(one level's target condition becomes the next lower level's challenge)

Using Kata to Roll Out TWI

The real benefit gained by the use of the Shepherding Groups is the learning that comes from the *failures* of Kata and the discoveries made when overcoming them. This learning and development create huge benefits for the organization at large and for the management system we are trying to create. We know that the application of the TWI skills will benefit the organization. But it goes, for the most part, underutilized unless we apply follow-up and coaching as done by the Shepherding Groups.

In addition to "Kata-ing the Kata," we have found using Kata indispensable to rolling out other parts of the management system, especially our TWI activities. Using this same approach, we have engaged the meta-process of Kata to guide and lock in practice of the TWI skills that need discipline and guidance if we want them to become a part of the daily culture. Obstacles to training – not enough trainers, no time to train, takes too long to train using JI, shortage of time, experienced operators' resist new techniques, cannot afford to waste supplies on training, jobs are too long to train, workers have no motivation to learn, jobs are too complex to train, etc. – will quickly hobble the most enthusiastic Job Instruction trainers as they struggle to find their feet. Simply teaching people the JI skill will not overcome these obstacles.

Kata Shepherding Groups help steer the step-by-step implementation and roll-out of the TWI skill use the Kata coaching cycles to experiment with counter-measures to overcome obstacles and ensure long-term success. By coaching the *process* of skill implementation, we set ourselves up for success in practicing the skills and reaping the benefits of their application. This, in turn, keeps us in line with our guiding principles of *Seek Perfection* and *Focus on Process*.

Conclusion – Empowerment Is Not Entitlement

In this chapter, we have stressed following the process and allowing the people who do the work to take ownership. We give guidance, by enforcing the process, making sure our people go in the right direction with the skills they need to solve their problems. It does not mean they are entitled to do anything they want. In fact, Peter Block, some years after he taught the management world about empowerment, warned, "entitlement is empower-ment run aground." He wrote:

> All the recent attention to empowerment has reinforced, uninten-tionally, our zeal for entitlement. Believing that now empowered we can do exactly what we want, and get all that we ask for, is simply trying to win at the new game. Doing our own thing is a self-serving act.[9]

Instead of entitlement, our management system must deploy meta-processes that guide us to a work environment that reflects our principles of respect and humility and help us work effectively as a unified organization. These processes allow for true empowerment to take place; they provide the

---

[9] Peter Block, *Stewardship: Choosing Service Over Self-Interest* (San Francisco, CA: Berrett-Koehler Publishers, Inc., 1993).

coaching and guidance to support our people as they take responsibility for advancing the strategies of the organization. Let's state again, "Empowerment is not abandonment."

What is your understanding of and attitude toward empowering your people with the skills and authority to take actions of their own volition to improve their working routines? How do you see your role in making sure they are successful in that effort? Being more conscious of your own behaviors is a good start. Recognize and release yourself from a command-and-control mindset. Reflection on the People principles of humility and respect for people can help ground you to take a new approach to carrying out Process.

Chapter 6

How We Do the Work

Once we have an effective way to see the work, developing a process that defines, guides, and improves on the work we do, then we have to follow that process. More than simply following the *Nike* phrase, Just Do It, we must Do It Right. That means practicing the scientific thinking model of experimenting to prove, or disprove, our hypotheses and allowing it to be OK to fail, as long as we fail safely and our learning from that failure propels us forward. By forward, we mean moving toward a "standard" way of working that we can lock into and use as our pattern of work, or, as we like to say, "how we play the game." We'll use this pattern until a better way is found and the current standard is upgraded to the new method. The key here, as we have been saying throughout, is sticking to the process.

In particular, when it comes to *doing* the work, we need to focus on how the elements of the system – programs, and methods we have put into our management system – interact, that all gears are effectively and efficiently spinning together, following our guiding principle to *Think Systemically*. A system, as we now know, is not just one thing or another that we do for its own sake, but a combination of things that, when and because they interact, create synergy and potential. Recognizing the importance of those interactions and developing their vitality is key. It is in the relationship between these various efforts that we expand our capability to address our challenges and to overcome the obstacles.

Make no mistake, we can and must develop mastery in all the individual programs and skills we want to deploy. But since our topic is management systems, not one individual program, let's focus on the interactions.[1] In Chapter 1, we talked about what those pieces might be and stated that each organization would have to find its own combination of "correct" system components. Let us remind you again, we are not trying to cover all the elements of a good management system or make a comprehensive list of the many possibilities. We are still learning what makes an effective management system. We have described some basic practices we have used in management systems: Policy Deployment (*Hoshin Kanri*), TWI, and Kata. So, let's jump right in and see how we coordinate and use these three system components so that the elements of the management system work well together.

TWI and Kata Play Well Together

When Kata was introduced and grew in the early 2010s, it was, perhaps, not too surprising that many TWI practitioners immediately recognized the symbiotic relationship between the two methodologies. First, both TWI and Kata emphasized practice over knowledge and laid out specific steps that could, through repetition, create true ability in the skills. Second, they were presented in practical terminology, not deep theory, to attract participation at all levels of any organization in any field or industry. Finally, while not "simplistic" in any way, they were fairly easy to apply and could obtain quick results that spurred rapid adaptation and dissemination. Much more than just these outward similarities, though, we have found profoundly meaningful the way the two methodologies complement each other to the point where, in the extreme, one cannot thrive completely and effectively without the other.

Remembering the history of TWI in Japan, this may not be so far fetched a notion. We know that when TWI was introduced into Toyota, Taiichi Ono, the founder of the Toyota Production System, was struggling to achieve standardized work practices (see insert: Taiichi Ono Searches for Standard Work). Only after he learned TWI's Job Instruction methodology was he able to document, and then promulgate, standardized work practices.[2] Since standardized work is the foundation of Toyota practice, and TWI continues

---

[1] Refer to the end of Chapter 1 for important books that teach the individual methods and skills we have referred to in this book.
[2] Lecture from Mr. Isao Kato in December of 2017.

to be used in Toyota today, we know that TWI had a large impact on the early development of *their management system*, the Toyota Production System, and its philosophical underpinnings. This is reflected in the pattern we today call Toyota Kata.

TAIICHI ONO SEARCHES FOR STANDARD WORK

In December of 2017, Patrick led a group of TWI trainers to Japan and visited Toyota City where they spent an afternoon with Mr. Isao Kato, the man responsible for training at Toyota beginning in the early 1950s. In this capacity, Kato worked directly with Taiichi Ono, the founder of the Toyota Production System (TPS), throughout its formative years. He gave our group this somewhat humorous account of Ono's search for Standard Work and the role TWI played in that process.

Taiichi Ono's inspiration for finding and enforcing standardized work, according to Kato, came in part from his frustration with always having to scramble at the end of each month to meet the monthly production targets. Ono thought about what the monthly targets were at the beginning of each month and that if the group produced a specific volume each day, it would not have to scramble for those targets at the very end of the month. In order to produce a specific volume each day, he continued to think about working to a set takt time, the time it takes to complete one cycle of the production line process, to ensure meeting the daily volume. In order to do that, they would have to have fixed procedures for each cycle of work so that it is done in the same, fixed amount of time each time, no matter who did it.

Ono's problem was that he did not know how the processes were done, what the laborers were doing to build the parts, and the workers would not tell him. At the time, just after the war ended and the Japanese economy was in a shambles, there was much labor strife in Toyota with layoffs and salary cuts; this led to a strike that almost bankrupted the company in 1950. Ono and his staff, then, to figure out the standard procedures, went into the factory at night, after all the experienced operators had gone home, and attempted to build the parts themselves. But they struggled to make quality parts and created a lot of scrap along the way. Because they didn't want the workers to know what they were doing, they had to hide these scrap parts somewhere they would not be found.

The old wooden factories of the time built large pools of water, not for swimming but in case the building caught on fire. Ono and his crew threw the scrap parts into the water where they could not be seen at the bottom of the pool. Much later, when the pool was drained for cleaning, all the scrap parts were discovered; the cleaners scratched their heads trying to figure out how they got there!

Kato explained how it was during this time of struggle, following the strike, that TWI was introduced to Toyota as a concession to the labor union, which was complaining about the poor quality of supervision. The human resources staff, Kato was keen to point out, were responsible for bringing in TWI, but Ono quickly became enamored with the Job Instruction portion of TWI as it gave him, *for the first time*, a means of writing down the standardized processes he was seeking in a fashion that could then be spread effectively to workers throughout the plant and, ultimately, the entire company. The JI format thus became embedded in the Toyota Production System at this very formative stage.

As a side note, while Job Relations also became a staple of TPS along with the JI method, Ono felt that the Job Methods portion of TWI, with its Eliminate – Combine – Rearrange – Simplify format, was a bit too simplistic for Toyota at that point. JM still had a large influence on TPS. When Mr. Kato began teaching JM classes six months after the introduction of JI, Ono remarked to him that, in Step 2 of the JM method, asking why a detail of the job was necessary *only once* would not get you to the answer. "It was I," Kato told us, "who went to Ono's office the next day with a proposal to answer his complaint. I told him, 'All right, we'll ask Why five times then!'" And that was the advent of the famous "Five Whys" in Toyota problem solving.

Let's look at how TWI and Kata work together. The Improvement Kata gives us the basic pattern of thinking so we decisively, step by step, experiment our way through the obstacles that separate our current condition from the next target condition we are striving to achieve, keeping in mind that there is a series of target conditions we must go through before reaching the challenge. The current condition is defined by three things: our process metrics, our results metrics, and our pattern of work, how we are "playing the game," with the process and results metrics manifestations of how we are playing the game. The target condition, which consists of the same three elements in hypothetical form, helps us navigate toward our challenge, which, in turn, is aligned with the overall vision of the organization (see Figure 6.1). This vision, along with the enterprise-wide goals directly emanating from the vision, comes from our Policy Deployment, as outlined in Chapter 2, and the Kata practice ensures that the activities we pursue on the front lines are aligned with this vision.

"Working on the work" or "improving the work" means overcoming the obstacles and devising ways to do the work better so that we get to our target conditions. We cannot assume that our people already have the ability to take down these obstacles, many of which will take real skill to overcome. Yet, as we discussed in last chapter, we do not want to tell them what to do, much less do it for them, so we must provide them with the skills to navigate through these treacherous waters. We can use Pareto Charts, Value Stream Maps, Cause-and-Effect Diagrams, etc., but this is where TWI comes into play. TWI provides the essential skills front-line leaders and coaches must have to guide their people to improvement.

When we run into obstacles, more often than not they will have something to do with *stability, productivity*, or the *working environment. Instability* of the working processes creates variation that adversely affects quality, output, safety, cost, etc. When we dig into our current condition, we inevitably find that people do the same job differently; even the same person may not do it the same way every time it is performed. With the best of intentions, this variation causes defects, accidents, and waste. Our TWI Job Instruction skill gives us a powerful countermeasure to this variability and can stabilize processes by creating a standardized method for "how we play the game."

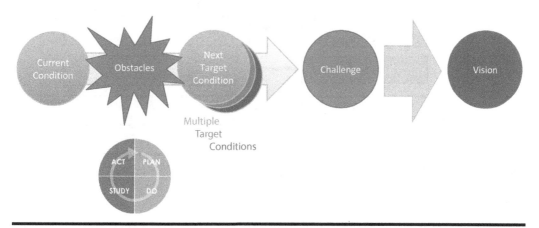

Figure 6.1   Improvement Kata Model

If the obstacle directly affects *productivity*, our Job Methods Improvement skill allows us to understand our current condition more thoroughly and come up with ideas to correct a sub-optimal process. Ideas from this JM activity are gained from the people actually doing the work so the resulting improvement is more likely to be implemented with good effect. Again, this follows our principles of respect and humility by not telling people what to do but giving them the skills to find answers on their own.

Finally, we can say that almost all obstacles contain some people component that needs to be addressed. A poor *working environment* will throw obstacles into our path almost every day of the week. As we discussed in depth in Chapter 3, Job Relations is the skill needed to create and maintain strong relationships and prevent further problems from occurring.

Figure 6.2 shows a representation of the Improvement Kata model integrated with the TWI skills.[3] While certainly not the totality of approaches we take in our Kata practice, these provide foundational skills that can address big obstacles. Moreover, this Kata thinking pattern, this meta-process, is an

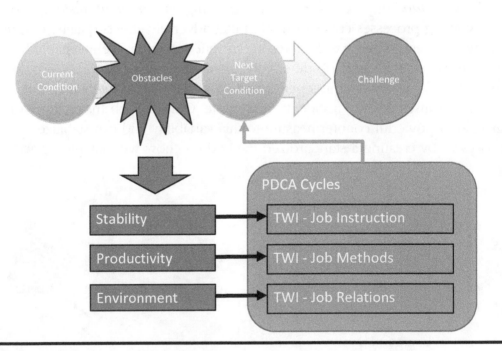

Figure 6.2   TWI & Kata Integration

[3] Thanks to Frank Gorena and his Op-Ex team at B/E Aerospace (now a division of Rockwell Collins Inc) for creating and sharing this model.

approach that can be taken whether we are dealing with the work of a front-line employee or the CEO of the organization.

In this way, the Improvement Kata and the Coaching Kata are like the "brain" of the management system while Policy Deployment is the "compass" that keeps us moving in the right direction, toward our "North Star" principles. Our TWI skills, and other practical pieces we put into play, are like the "gasoline" that keeps the motor turning and makes the whole thing run. These are the "small gears" we saw at the bottom of our Gear Train Model. In a real mechanical gear train, the power from the motor is distributed from the smallest to the rest of the gears to "reduce" the process speed so the system doesn't burn out. Our system's "energy" truly emanates from the "small gears." Our improvement process hums when they interact well with the other gears in the systems.

Manufacturing Example of TWI and Kata

Let's outline a hypothetical example to illustrate this pattern covering the breadth of the TWI-Kata relationship. Let's say a small plant with a few process lines had the challenge of increasing its productivity by 50% in one year's time. As a target condition to be achieved by month's end, they set out to stabilize daily output to 95% of the standard when their current condition was daily output fluctuating between 80–105% of the standard. This fluctuation, they determined, was a core cause for chronic low productivity. The current obstacle is that the process in Station A, at the beginning of the production process, is unstable, causing most of the fluctuation in daily output as delays here ripple throughout the entire line. A simplified version of the Kata Storyboard, showing only these details (there are always many, many more on an actual board), is shown in Figure 6.3.

In their first PDSA cycle, after reconfirming the current and target conditions, the coach confirmed that the learner was working on the obstacle of instability in Station A and asked what her next step, her next experiment, would be. Since there is a lot of variation in Station A's work causing the gap from where they are to where they want to be with daily output, her idea was to use Job Instruction to stabilize and then standardize the work with the operator. She felt this would be a good experiment and help maintain a takt time[4] of 45 seconds.

---

[4] Takt time is the rate at which a finished product needs to be completed in order to meet customer demand.

Focus Process: XYZ Line		Challenge: Increase productivity 50%
Target Condition Achieve by: Month end Stabilize daily output to >95% of standard	**Actual Condition Now** Output fluctuates daily between 80-105% of standard	**PDCA Record**
		Obstacles Parking Lot Process at Station A is unstable

Figure 6.3 Kata Storyboard

The next question in the coaching Kata would be, "What do you expect (from this next step)?" Her expectation was that the operator would work steadily at the prescribed takt time (see Figure 6.4). Then, "How quickly can we see what we have learned from taking that step?" She felt she could break down the job for training and provide instruction that afternoon, in other words, use JI to create a standard of behavior, so the following day would be a good time to come back and see how it's going.

After instructing the operator how to perform the job in Station A to create a standard of performance, the next coaching cycle, carried out the next day, took place to reflect on this last step to see if the learner's hypothesis held true. She hypothesized that if there were good job instruction, the variation would go away. What actually happened, though, in spite of all her good efforts, is that the operator's work continued to be unstable, slowing down productivity and not meeting the takt time. When asked by her coach what she had learned, the learner stated that the problem was, in fact, not the operator's skill, but his willingness to follow and stick to the standard. She was an experienced JI instructor and knew the instruction method worked in developing standardized work. Therefore, the problem must be with the operator's attitude.

When asked by her coach what her next step would be, the learner considered applying the foundations for good relations (praising the worker and giving him a chance to share his "opinions and feelings" about the work) that come with the TWI Job Relations skill. She replied that she expected the

PDSA CYCLES RECORD *(Each row = one experiment)*						
Obstacle: **Process at Station A is Unstable**		Process: **XYZ Line**				
		Learner: **Bill**			Coach: **Mary**	
Date, step, & metric	What do you expect?	Do a Coaching Cycle	Conduct the Experiment	What happened		What we learned
April 11, 20XX Train Operator on standard work operation using JI. *Maintain tact time of 45 seconds.*	The Operator will work steadily at prescribed tact time.					

Figure 6.4   1st PDSA Cycle

operator, given a chance to unload his true feelings, would make a variety of complaints about the company and the working conditions. Nevertheless, she thought that giving him a chance to vent would be a good first step toward rebuilding cooperation and trust. She thought that he might not come right out with these confessions, so when asked by her coach when they could go and check on the results, she thought they might have to give it a few days. Figure 6.5 shows the PDSA cycle board with this second round.

Moving on to the 3rd PDSA cycle: After a few days of working on Job Relations with the operator, although the learner had expected the operator to have many complaints, to her surprise he said that he was trying hard to perform the job following the defined procedure he had been taught. The reason he could not maintain the takt time, he explained, was that the tool he used to perform the task was heavy and difficult to handle in the confined workspace of Station A. Moreover, the operator confirmed that he was hesitant to complain about the difficulty he was having, fearing it would jeopardize his job, which he liked and needed. What she learned from the

PDSA CYCLES RECORD (*Each row = one experiment*)

Obstacle: **Process at Station A is Unstable**		Process: **XYZ Line**		
		Learner: **Bill**		Coach: **Mary**
Date, step, & metric	What do you expect?		What happened	What we learned
April 11, 20XX Train Operator on standard work operation using JI. *Maintain tact time of 45 seconds.*	The Operator will work steadily at prescribed tact time.		The Operator's work time continues to be unstable and slows down productivity.	The problem is not the Operator's skill but his willingness to follow the standard.
April 12, 20XX Use JR Foundations to praise Operator and solicit opinions. *Better cooperation.*	The Operator will bring out a variety of complaints about the company and working conditions.			

(Vertical column labels between "expect?" and "What happened": Do a Coaching Cycle | Conduct the Experiment)

Figure 6.5   2nd PDSA Cycle

experiment is that she shouldn't be so quick to judge the operator's reasons not to follow instructions and to get the facts before jumping to a conclusion. She also learned that it was quite beneficial to take the time to talk with the operator to bring the truth to light.

The next PDSA experiment was a no-brainer – use TWI's Job Methods Improvement skill to analyze the current working method and find a better procedure for handling the tool to reduce fatigue and work more comfortably in the confined space. What she expected was that the operator would cooperate in coming up with an improved method because he understood the difficult conditions and was motivated to make it better. She felt that it might take several days to devise and test an improved method so the coach and learner decided to have their next coaching session early the following week. Figure 6.6 shows the PDSA cycle board with this third round.

In the 4th PDSA cycle, the learner, working with the operator, designed a jig, a mechanical device, to hold the heavy tool and rearranged the work

PDSA CYCLES RECORD *(Each row = one experiment)*					
Obstacle: **Process at Station A is Unstable**		Process: **XYZ Line**			
			Learner: **Bill**		Coach: **Mary**
Date, step, & metric	What do you expect?			What happened	What we learned
April 11, 20XX Train Operator on standard work operation using JI. *Maintain tact time of 45 seconds.*	The Operator will work steadily at prescribed tact time.			The Operator's work time continues to be unstable and slows down productivity.	The problem is not the Operator's skill but his willingness to follow the standard.
April 12, 20XX Use JR Foundations to praise Operator and solicit opinions. *Better cooperation.*	The Operator will bring out a variety of complaints about the company and working conditions.	Do a Coaching Cycle	Conduct the Experiment	Operator pointed out how tiring it was to handle the heavy tool in a confined work space.	Shouldn't be so quick to question Operator's motives. But talking helped bring out the true conditions.
April 15, 20XX Find better working procedure using JM to handle heavy tool. *Reduce fatigue.*	The Operator will engage in coming up with a better method.				

Figure 6.6   3rd PDSA Cycle

sequence to reduce the amount of time the operator held the tool. She learned from this experiment that there were many more improvements to be found beyond fixing the immediate problem at hand. The next experiment would be to return to our Job Instruction skill, break down the new method for training, and train the operator. She expected good cooperation from the operator in learning and following the new method since he contributed to making it; she believed that the process would be able to hold to the takt time.

Sure enough, in the 5th PDSA cycle, the learner reported that, after giving the training and running the new method for six hours until the end of the shift, the operator was able to maintain the takt time and keep up with the standard output. She learned, in reaching this target condition, that it took a combination of all three TWI skills: Job Instruction, Job Relations, and Job Methods Improvement to overcome the obstacle of variation in Process A. Figure 6.7 shows these 4th and 5th PDSA cycles.

PDSA CYCLES RECORD *(Each row = one experiment)*					
Obstacle: Process at Station A is Unstable		Process: **XYZ Line**			
		Learner: **Bill**			Coach: **Mary**
Date, step, & metric	**What do you expect?**			**What happened**	**What we learned**
April 11, 20XX Train Operator on standard work operation using JI. *Maintain tact time of 45 seconds.*	The Operator will work steadily at prescribed tact time.			The Operator's work time continues to be unstable and slows down productivity.	The problem is not the Operator's skill but his willingness to follow the standard.
April 12, 20XX Use JR Foundations to praise Operator and solicit opinions. *Better cooperation.*	The Operator will bring out a variety of complaints about the company and working conditions.	Do a Coaching Cycle	Conduct the Experiment	Operator pointed out how tiring it was to handle the heavy tool in a confined work space.	Shouldn't be so quick to question Operator's motives. But talking helped bring out the true conditions.
April 15, 20XX Find better working procedure using JM to handle heavy tool. *Reduce fatigue.*	The Operator will engage in coming up with a better method.			Created jig to hold tool and rearranged work sequence to reduce holding time.	Found more improvements than expected even after we improved the problem point.
April 20, 20XX Breakdown new method and train again using JI. *Maintain tact time.*	Good cooperation from Operator in learning the new method since he contributed to it.			Maintained tact time and productivity for 6 hours until end of shift.	Moving toward the target condition was a combination of all three TWI Skills: JI, JR, and JM.

Figure 6.7   4th and 5th PDSA Cycles

Healthcare Example of TWI and Kata

Here is an actual example from a hospital; it represents the principles of connectivity between TWI and Kata we saw in the last idealized manufacturing example. It is a little "messier," but now that we have a clear idea of the pattern, we can see what that looks like in real life.

As a high-level strategy, a large hospital serving a wide rural area wanted to improve its patient service and satisfaction scores, which have a large impact on reimbursement rates and the overall financial health of the institution. The hospital saw room for improvement in the Emergency Department (ED), which was seeing a rapid increase in the number of patients.

The current condition in the ED was that, for the previous fiscal year, they showed a total Length of Stay (LOS) of 172.75 minutes for patients who were discharged from the ED (i.e., they were not admitted to the hospital directly from the ED but were sent home). More critically, the rate of patients who

Left Without Being Seen (LWBS) was at 24%, a very poor rate that meant that patients were giving up on the long wait and either going home or moving to other healthcare facilities, facilities like Urgent Care Centers that compete with the hospital for patients. Once in the ED, the time from entering the door to seeing a provider (doctor or nurse practitioner) was 54 minutes. The time from getting the disposition to departure was 32 minutes.

Some other details in the current condition, the pattern of work, included lack of consistency in nurses using protocols to begin testing and treatment in triage (the process of evaluating incoming patients on the level of their need for medical attention and determining priority). These triage nurses have set rules, or protocols, with which, depending on how the patient is presenting, they can begin blood tests or drugs *before* patients are seen by the doctor. In addition to this, there was inconsistency in communication between the ED nurses and staff in other related departments like radiology. Turnaround time for a plain x-ray was 27 minutes, and for a CT scan it was 57 minutes; they didn't know how much of that was waiting time.

Their challenge over the next three months was to get the LOS to 160 minutes or less and the LWBS to less than 2%. They also wanted to have clear and consistent communication, based on defined processes, with the patients and their families during the stay. They set as their target condition reducing "door to provider" time by ten minutes because this was something they could affect right away without having to engage the physicians (more on this at the end of the example). The obstacle they decided to work on first was stabilizing the triage process, as variation here affected not only waiting time up front but also waiting time after the patient was sent from the waiting room back to an examination room with the physician.

Job Methods was used to analyze the current method, which entailed one triage nurse interviewing an ED patient in a triage room and then applying any protocols she or he deemed necessary. Remember that currently protocols were not applied consistently and, when interviewed, several of the triage nurses didn't even know what the protocols were or where they could be researched. After questioning the details, ideas came out to *combine* the preliminary blood work collection, based on the protocols, and the patient interview, to do these two processes *at the same time* in two-person teams. Triage nurses must ask and document a list of questions, called Triage Part 1, in the Electronic Medical Records (EMR), so their hands are tied up at the computer during the interview. The proposal was that while Nurse #1, the documenter, is talking to the patient and inputting the answers into the EMR system, Nurse #2, the doer, could be drawing blood and getting samples off to the lab for testing. When these protocols were performed more consistently, it would have the added benefit of saving time *after* the patient went back to the examination room since lab results would be ready for the doctor during the examination, eliminating more waiting time.

It was immediately apparent upon drawing up the Proposed Method that we would need Job Instruction to teach the triage nurses to perform the two-person teamwork. The new method required the nurses to know how to do both jobs since they would rotate back and forth between documenting the interview and drawing the blood, depending on which job finished first. For example, if Nurse #1 finished first she would then go and get the next patient waiting for triage or, if there was no one in line, help in another triage room. If she finished last, she would transport the patient and clean the room. The same sequence would hold for Nurse #2 if he finished first or last.

Of course, the triage nurses already knew how to do the interview and the blood draw, but the new skill was all about getting down the coordination. When put into practice, the combined process worked like a dance and that needed instruction and practice if the teams were to work together well. So we made two Job Instruction Breakdowns (JIB), one for each job (see Figures 6.8 and 6.9) and taught both jobs to each of the triage nurses on the day shift as an "experiment" to see if the process would work.

We learned that it was difficult to train because the two processes were interconnected in sequence. Nurse #2's process does not even begin until Step 4, order protocols, of Nurse #1's process. Step 6 of Nurse #1's job, document IV and lab draw, cannot be done until Step 3, send blood to lab, of Nurse #2's process is complete. The way we handled the instruction was to teach in pairs, teaching Nurse #2's job first, since this process was dependent on the other, and having that nurse then role play the "doer's" work while teaching Nurse #1's job, the "documenter," to the other person in the pair being trained. Then we switched and taught the two jobs again to the same two nurses, the other way around. By the time they had gone through all the JI teaching cycles, they had the procedure pretty much down.

When we started practicing the process on real patients, though, it did not take long for the new method to fall apart. By definition, ED nurses are Type A personalities working in a frantic environment. When patients lining up for triage started to back up, they had difficulty "staying with the pattern" and went, almost by instinct, into fire-fighting mode. They later claimed that the teamwork was fine when there was time to adequately run the process, but when the pressure was on, and sick patients were waiting to be seen, they

JOB INSTRUCTION BREAKDOWN SHEET

Task: <u>Triage (2-person team) – Nurse #1 (Documenter)</u>

IMPORTANT STEPS	KEY POINTS
A logical segment of the operation when something happens to advance the work.	Anything in a step that might – 1. Make or break the job 2. Injure the worker 3. Make the work easier to do (i.e., "knack," "trick," special timing, bit of special information)
1. Get patient and enter chief complaint	1. Check identifiers 2. Ask while walking
2. Start vitals	1. Cuff first 2. Check restrictions
3. Start Triage Part 1	1. Assess and enter activity
4. Order protocols	1. Review list 2. Check appropriate boxes
5. Print & retrieve labels	1. Check for correct patient
6. Document IV & lab draw	1. Note who started IV 2. Make sure blood in tubes, then scan
7. Complete Triage Part 1 and proceed to next patient	1. Finish first – go get next patient or help another room 2. Finish last – transport patient and clean room

Figure 6.8   JIB for Triage Nurse #1

had to "keep the wheel turning," as one triage nurse put it. Here we realized we would need the full force of our Job Relations skill to build support and cooperation for the new method, which we knew would allow more patients to be triaged, not less. Trust had to be built in both our methods and intentions for them to believe that the new method was best for everyone in the long run.

After listening to their opinions and feelings, and there were a few who insisted there was "no way" this would work when patients backed up, we agreed to set a specified number of patients who would be waiting in line before they could "pull the plug" and go back to individually triaging patients. In this way, the triage nurses could manage their anxiety, knowing that things would not go "off the rails" because they were being forced to stick to a process they didn't fully trust. At the same time, it gave us a chance

JOB INSTRUCTION BREAKDOWN SHEET

Task: <u>Triage (2-person team) – Nurse #2 (Doer)</u>

IMPORTANT STEPS	KEY POINTS
A logical segment of the operation when something happens to advance the work.	Anything in a step that might – 1. Make or break the job 2. Injure the worker 3. Make the work easier to do (i.e., "knack," "trick," special timing, bit of special information)
1. Confirm instructions & get supplies	N/A
2. Perform tests	1. IV – 20 gage in AC 2. No more than 2 attempts 3. Draw a rainbow[1]
3. Send blood to lab	1. Check 2 patient identifiers via labels
4. Check with Nurse #1	1. Anything missing 2. Additional instructions
5. Proceed to next patient	1. Finish first – go get next patient or help another room 2. Finish last – transport patient and clean room

[1] Nurse jargon for filling all tubes. Different blood tests are distinguished by different color caps on the tubes. Here we want to fill all the colors, the "rainbow," because we don't know which tests will be needed later by the physician.

Figure 6.9   JIB for Triage Nurse #2

to have them practice and become comfortable with the team method, at least up to a certain point before they "pulled the plug." With that, it wasn't long before they settled into the new method, and these very same nurses began to complain that the weekend ED shifts, who were the last to be trained in the new method, were not "following the process."

Notice the iterations described here, the many experiments that were run before settling into the final procedure. This is the essence of real process change for critical processes in any organization, but especially in healthcare. The tools of our management system helped us to recognize and value this as a critical sequence of learning for our teams.

Over the next four months, there was a 50-minute reduction in LOS, and after six months, when comprehensive data was collected, discharge LOS stabilized at 141 minutes, well below their target of less than 160 minutes. The LWBS rate was 1.19%, meeting their target of less than 2% and well below the 24% for the period of time when the project was undertaken. Their target of reducing "door to provider" time by 10 minutes was met as they went from

54 minutes to 33 minutes. The improvement of the triage process resulted in the reduction of waiting time as well as a higher quality of care.

We explained in Chapter 1 how the three TWI methods work together. As we see here and in our theoretical manufacturing example, it takes a combination of the three TWI programs (JM, JI, and JR) skills to thoroughly manage our way around big obstacles of process and people. Our Kata mindset of experimenting our way forward gives us good guidance on where and when to apply these essential skills.

As a postscript to this story, it must be pointed out that the two-person triage work was not the only experiment we ran on getting to our challenge of reducing patient time in the ED. At about the same time, we conducted a JM project, having the provider, a doctor or nurse practitioner, treat lower-acuity patients right there in the triage area. This meant having the provider move out of the standard ED examination rooms to see low-acuity patients while they were sitting in the triage room, a room with privacy and basic equipment much like any examination room. These patients, who did not need extensive care or possible hospital admission, could then be sent home directly from triage without having to wait again, after triage, to be moved to an examination room. It also freed up examination rooms, which, when completely full, became another reason for long waiting times.

USING JM TO GET THE CURRENT CONDITION

One interesting benefit of introducing Job Methods into a Kata environment is that practitioners saw the value of using JM's Step 1, Break Down the Job, where you "list all details of the job exactly as done in the Current Method," as an excellent means of bringing out the current condition for their Kata storyboard. The JM breakdown articulates clearly the pattern of work currently being performed. Standard Kata practice uses the Block Diagram to quickly lay out the "big pieces" of the process as it is currently done, but applying this JM skill can give it more depth and detail. Many Kata coaches now begin any Kata project with a JM analysis of the current condition, which must be done at the gemba and not at one's desk. Because this part of the JM method has already been completed, it is simple and straight forward to continue using the JM method down the road as they overcome obstacles through improvement of the process. Some coaches will even complete the full 4-step JM process and use the new proposed method as their first target condition.

We mentioned earlier getting physicians participating in kaizen activities; quite honestly, this is one of our biggest challenges in healthcare. We discuss it here because this new process was a radical change from how ED physicians had always practiced, and we were expecting strong pushback. But by having one of the doctors who was interested in healthcare productivity help us design the system, we were able to adjust our ideas to fit the physician concerns (despite many difficult issues that needed addressing). When we trialed the process the next day for a full shift with another physician, it worked well. She had nothing but praise for the new way of seeing these non-critical patients right there in the triage area.

The Training Timetable

When it comes to getting the work done, the Training Timetable, which comes with the Job Instruction Method, is underappreciated and chronically underutilized. At its most basic level, this tool is a simple "skills matrix" showing who can do which job (see Figure 6.10), but it can be so much

JOB INSTRUCTION TRAINING TIMETABLE

Name: Debbie Jones Dept.: ICU Date: March 23, 2018	Breakdown No.	Donna G.	Mary K.	Billy B.	Sarah L.	Janie S.	Joe T.	Bobbie K.				Changes in Schedule
Hand hygiene – soap & water	001	✓	✓	✓	✓	✓	★	✓				
Hand hygiene – gel	002	✓	✓	✓	✓	✓	★	✓				
Scrub the hub	003	✓	✓	✓	✓	✓	✓					
Central line dressing change	004	✓	✓	✓	3/28	3/28	3/30	4/3				Updated procedure
Replace stat-lock	005	✓	✓	✓	★	✓	✓					
Catheter care	006	✓	4/5	4/10	✓	4/5	4/10	4/12				Updated procedure
Changing connectors	007	✓	✓									Testing new procedure
Turnover **Work Performance**					Struggles with stat-lock change		Needs refresher H.H. training	New staff member				

Figure 6.10 Training Timetable

more when used as a planning tool for making sure we always have capable people ready to handle the jobs that need to be done.

When Skip was an operations manager for a 1,000+ person plant making high-end components for the HVAC (air conditioning) industry, his facility had a tool center that stored millions of dollars' worth of specialty bits and cutters. The valuable tools were kept under "lock and key," meted out to the different manufacturing machines each shift by a skilled person who was familiar with all the plant processes. Because the plant was in the Midwest, each year they faced things like ice storms and heavy snow, not to mention people getting sick or other adverse circumstances. As operations manager, though, Skip could not tell headquarters "no production took place yesterday because the tool crib person was out." To deal with these situations, he managed his people in a way that ensured there was always someone available to run the tool center or any other part of the production process. While at the time he did not call it a Training Timetable, he had such a tool that helped him manage this very important priority.

In healthcare, a nursing department manager was overheard saying, "I'm worried because I don't have any heart nurses for this weekend." "What are you going to do?" we asked. She didn't have an answer but continued looking worried. In a different case, a patient came into the ED with a bad pacemaker and none of the nurses on shift that day knew how to deal with it because it was such a rare problem. The ED manager, who had not done the procedure in over ten years, was forced to fix it because no one else was available. This happens far too often in healthcare. When asking clinical professionals what they do when they must perform procedures they have not done in a long time, even dedicated super-smart healthcare workers say, quietly, "We try to remember the training we had, however long ago it was."

This begs the question of how we do training and how we plan for that training. A typical approach is to "shadow" an experienced person and watch until you can do it for yourself. This approach, as is discussed at length in other TWI works,[5] is fraught with problems and leads to poor outcomes in quality, safety, and productivity because of the variation and instability in the work processes left behind by the practice. In the worst case, disaster can happen when employees are injured or killed because of poor skills or when major quality issues occur with the final product or service that is delivered

---

[5] See Patrick Graupp and Robert J. Wrona, *The TWI Workbook: Essential Skills for Supervisors*, 2nd Edition (Boca Raton, FL: CRC Press, 2016).

to the customer. In healthcare, the safety and health, not to mention the lives, of the patients we care for are put at risk.

Developing the working skills of our people is the vital role of Job Instruction and is effectively managed using the Training Timetable. Here we can quickly and effectively find our urgent training needs and then apply good job instruction to fill those gaps by determining who we need to train, for which job, and by what date. In Chapter 2, we saw a healthcare example concerning the alignment of front-line work to prevent CLABSI and CAUTI in-hospital infections. We saw how success in training would directly lead to reaching hospital-wide goals of reducing infection rates. Once we determined that training can standardize procedures like Central Line Dressing Change and Catheter Care, which will reduce the variation in these procedures that can allow infections to set in, we set up the Training Timetable to plan and direct the successful training delivery. Figure 6.10 shows the Training Timetable for an ICU unit training these jobs and a few other jobs directly connected to infection control.

The Training Timetable is an invaluable way to bring the needed skillsets of the department into visual management and shows, at a glance, what skills are available at any given time according to who is on the job and what each of them can do. Using this tool, any shift supervisor can manage the skills of his or her work team ensuring that proper training is given and there are no "gaps" in needed capabilities. It is also a great way to engage teams in the critical skillsets needed to efficiently manage departments. Seeing gaps on the Training Timetable posted on the department's huddle board is a great way for leaders to identify needs in advance and get support for needed training.

Training Timetables and Process Confirmation[6]

A critical aspect of good Job Instruction is the follow-up process that ensures operators and staff are performing jobs to the standard taught in the training. Even though learners have shown, in the JI instruction, that they can perform a specific task following the standard and know the reasons to do it that way, it is human nature to fall back on old habits. Embedded in the JI method is a series of repetitions of doing the work, performed by the learner during the

---

[6] Thanks to Judy Mann at Baptist Memorial Hospital Memphis for this great example. Judy and her team have also been instrumental in using Kata to roll out their TWI implementation as mentioned at the end of the last chapter.

TWI Training Schedule

JIB: Foley Insertion

Unit: ICU

Trainer: Joyce Bing (JB)

Skill Level

Level 1 - NOVICE: Beginning Level of Skill

Level 2 - ADVANCED BEGINNER: Moderate Level of Skill Development

Level 3 - COMPETENT: High Level of Skill Development

Level 4- PROFICIENT: Meets Level 3 and Can Train Others

Date of Training	Staff Name	Initial Train Time	Verification		Validation				Validation	
			Level	Trainer	Quarter 1	Q1 Level	Quarter 2	Q2 Level	Quarter 3	Q3 Level
4/18/2017	Judy Nurse	45 min	2	JB	7/1/2017 JB	2	9/26/17 JB	3	1/5/18 JB	3
4/21/2017	Samuel Parker	32 min	3	Jackie Parton	7/2/2017 JB	2	9/26/17 JB	2	1/6/18 JB	3
4/24/2017	Dianne Jackson	43 min	1	JB	7/6/2017 JB	2	10/1/17 JB	2	1/10/18 JB	3
4/28/2017	Sarah Brown	38 min	2	JB	7/24/2017 Jackie P	3	10/6/17 Jackie P	3	1/18/18 JB	2
4/30/2017	Jodie Crown	48 min	1	JB	7/25/2018 JB	2	10/9/17 JB	2	1/19/18 JB	2
5/2/2017	Laura Sanders	41 min	1	JB	7/25/2018 JB	1	10/21/17 JB	2	1/25/18 JB	2
5/3/2017	Theresa Needles	37 min	3	Jackie Parton	8/1/2017 JB	3	11/1/17 JB	2	1/31/18 Jackie P	3

Figure 6.11   Training Timetable with Quarterly Validation and Skill Level Grading

Job Instruction process, to help create the new habit, but inevitably it takes time after beginning to perform the job alone for the pattern to be fully ingrained, to be "hard wired," as we like to say in healthcare.

Many organizations have modified their Training Timetables to assist in this follow-up process by using them like a control sheet for job audits and process confirmation. The timetable will show not only the date the training takes place, but also the dates, and perhaps results, of the follow-up checks to determine when the person is "signed-off" and fully capable of doing the job. Figure 6.11 shows an example of a Training Timetable for just one job, Foley insertion, the most common type of urinary catheter; you can see that after the initial training for each nurse was completed, a *verification* was made in the next week to a month to ensure the trained nurse was correctly and consistently using the method. Then, the trainer performed quarterly *validations* to make sure the nurses had not fallen back on their old ways or changed the standard.

Training Timetables for New Workers

We consistently get feedback data, across all industries, on the time it takes to bring new people up to full speed on the job. For example, if it used to take four weeks to get a new worker fully capable of doing work, with Job Instruction that time has now shrunk to five days. These numbers are easy to track, and many plants, hospitals, and service centers have good records that are verifiable. It is not surprising to see reductions of up to 75%. One manufacturer of custom windows, which entailed a lot of craftsmen-type jobs with wood frames, ran an experiment of sending two new workers out for training, one with JI and one under the traditional training method. Under the old method, the new worker took 160 hours to get up to speed, and the supervisor was still "not fully certain" that he could do everything correctly. With JI, in less than 60 hours the supervisor was 100% confident the learner had mastered the job. At a call center for a school supply distribution company that ships to teachers all across the country, Job Instruction was able to reduce the training time of new service representatives from three days to two hours!

Here the Training Timetable can help organize the training of new employees in a way that builds on skills taught one at a time over a fixed period. Workers can then practice and master the basic skills before moving on to the more advanced ones, the result being they move up the learning curve much more quickly. In other words, instead of just sending a new worker out to "job shadow" experienced employees and try to figure out the entire routine over many days, or weeks, we can plan for their training in a strategic manner that identifies the most basic skills of the job and teaches them one by one as they increase in complexity, building on the experience and knowledge they gain along the way. What is more, these new workers can begin to work productively almost immediately, not necessarily doing the entirety of the job right off the bat, but certainly not just hanging around watching other people work for days or weeks at a time.

Figure 6.12 shows just such a Training Timetable for a new material handler in a warehouse. Notice that this timetable shows how one "Job Duty" can contain multiple "Instructional Units," which means there will be several Job Instruction Breakdowns to be taught to fully master that particular part of the job. In this way, the Training Timetable helps us to take large jobs, or jobs that take a long time to do, and divide them up into smaller "bite size" chunks that can be learned piece by piece. This follows the

Job Instruction Training Timetable						
Name: Johnny Green Position: Material Handler	Plant/Location: Chemical Division Department: Mixing		Instructor: Joe Trainer Supervisor: Jane Leader			
Job Duties	**Instructional Units**	**Time Intervals** (how quickly can you train this person?)				
List jobs you need this person to learn	List the associated breakdown sheets for each Job Duty	Day 1	Day 2	Day 3	Day 4	Day 5
Operating Forklift	Operating cabin controls	X				
	Navigating	X				
	Lifting/lowering	X				
	Navigating with load	X				
Forklift maintenance and care	Charging the forklift		X			
	Preventative maintenance		X			
Replenishment of raw materials and supplies	Replenishment of primary mix			X		
	Replenishment of secondary mix				X	
	Replenishment of mixing supplies					X
	Reordering materials with barcode		X			
Running the "C" route	Replenishment of zones C1			X		
	Replenishment of zones C2-C4			X		
	Replenishment of zones C5-C9			X		
Running the "F" route	Replenishment of zones F1-F3					X
	Replenishment of zones F4-F8					X
Evaluation of employee progress:	*This employee learned rapidly and has a fine attitude.*					
		Signature		*Joe Trainer*		

Figure 6.12 Training Timetable for a New Operator

instruction principle, taught in JI, of not giving a person more information than can be handled at one time. This approach speeds up the overall training time.

Training Timetables and Rare Jobs

A common issue that comes up with training concerns jobs that are rarely, if ever, performed, as we saw earlier when the ED manager had to deal with a failing pacemaker. For rare diseases, like Ebola, we must be prepared, especially if your hospital is picked as the designated treatment site in your city. In a factory or office, there are times when machinery breaks down (e.g., paper jams in the copy machine), and we would be better served by fixing it ourselves rather than waiting for the maintenance crew to show up. There may be special models or requests in production that are both rare and small in number but must still be attended to.

The Training Timetable can be used to keep track of when employees have had the opportunity to perform these rare or infrequent procedures; we can then provide timely training using the Job Instruction method of repetition and practice. For example, if we think a person should perform a certain task at least once in a three-month period to retain proficiency, then we would give refresher training if he or she has gone three months without doing it. Our Training Timetable can keep track of that work activity. Because the Job Instruction Method includes the learner's performing the job several times, we can use the training method as a means of getting "hands-on" practice for a task that, by definition, only rarely comes around.

Good hospitals have "training lab" facilities stocked with expensive training equipment like mannequins that talk, breathe, and bleed. Some manufacturing plants have what they call the "training dojo" with actual reproductions of workstations or even working assembly lines. Are these facilities being utilized optimally for training other than basic skills? We recommend using these facilities much more frequently on a regular basis for training experienced workers on jobs that are done rarely so that their skills are fresh when they are called upon to do them.

Conclusion – Balancing People and Process

In these last two chapters, we have focused on how we see and do the work of the enterprise. Doing the work is all about managing the process, after you have put the right elements of your management system in place, and allowing the people to manage their own work following that process. Guiding and coaching people to success is the truest role of management.

What is your management system? That is something only you, and your management team, can decide. The only thing we can do here in is describe how those pieces, those gears, you put into place must work together smoothly and effectively. If your transmission is humming, your engine will shift smoothly into the gears you need for your car to take you wherever you need to go, safely and efficiently. When the various components of your management system function well together, the synergy created will deliver the results your organization needs and desires.

In all these efforts, the proper balance of the scientific thinking, the gears, and the humanistic factors, the lubrication, must be kept in check. We saw in Chapters 3 and 4 how vital it is to take the proper approach in dealing with people and how, in the end, that is determined primarily by our ability to manage ourselves. In Chapters 5 and 6, we saw how an organization built on trust and strong relationships can leverage the true value of all its people by empowering them to deliver, at every level, the performance needed to reach its goals. With good balance between our People and our Process, and with guiding direction from our Purpose, we will be getting closer to finding the right formula for a successful management system.

Commanding Results

4

Chapter 7

Staying on Track

The purpose of the management system is to leverage the outcomes of our daily practices to create value for the customer. When the right components are properly aligned in the right configuration and are running smoothly (because they are well "lubricated" by strong human relationships), the synergy, or "inherent energy," of the entire system creates quality at each point in the production/patient care/service process. In the Introduction, when we first introduced the Gear Train Model, we pointed out what are called "Locked in Loads" that create additional energy over and above what is coming from the power source. This is the result of the spring reaction that comes from the interaction of the component parts as they stretch and flex. In the same way, when people are working well together as a motivated team with common purpose, they "stretch and flex" in ways that even they, much less the organization, could not imagine they would, or could, ever perform. This synergy delivers quality in performance that goes way beyond "business as usual" and follows our guiding principle to *Create Value for the Customer*.

Peter Senge, in his landmark book on Learning Organizations, *The Fifth Discipline*, described being on a team where this kind of profound synergy took place:

> Most of us at one time or another have been part of a great "team,"
> a group of people who functioned together in an extraordinary
> way – who trusted one another, who complemented each others'

strengths and compensated for each others' limitations, who had common goals that were larger than individual goals, and who produced extraordinary results. I have met many people who have experienced this sort of profound teamwork – in sports, or in the performing arts, or in business. Many say that they have spent much of their life looking for that experience again.[1]

What if we developed management systems that create an environment that provide people with the opportunity, day in and day out, to fulfill that dream, the lifelong search for deep meaning in something bigger than ourselves? Senge calls that a Learning Organization; Toyota calls it the Toyota Production System, and Amazon calls it We Pioneer. We could just call it Continuous Improvement. In a sense, as human beings, we are all searching for something that lifts us far above any place we could ever go on our own. Our job is to provide the pathway for all of us to get there. When we do that, there will be little need to look at the scoreboard because, as we revel in self-fulfillment, we will be providing unparalleled value and quality to our customers.

Entropy and the Sand Castle

In the summer of 2017, after huge progress had been made since his hospital had introduced the new management system thinking in 2014, Brad was having a discussion with one of his nurse managers. She confessed, "Mr. Parsons, what we are doing is great. We can see our gaps and people are engaged. But, you know, it requires a lot of effort and it would be much easier to go back to command-and-control!" This comment made it clear to him the fragile nature of a management system and the difficulty of building sustainability.

The second law of thermodynamics tells us that the state of entropy, or disorder, of the entire universe will increase over time. When left to their own devices in a closed system, energy and matter will deteriorate, degrade, decompose, and degenerate in a gradual decline into disorder. This is why, when we put an ice cube on the table, it melts. It's why whenever we clean

[1] Peter Senge, *The Fifth Discipline: The Art & Practice of the Learning Organization* (New York, NY: Currency Doubleday, 1990).

a room it gets messy again. It's why we get older, never younger. It's also why the management system we put into place, no matter how skillfully and successfully it is done, will deteriorate over time. Peter Drucker, the management guru who literally wrote the book on Management, said, "Only three things happen naturally in organizations: friction, confusion, and underperformance. Everything else requires leadership."

How do we manage Purpose, People, and Process, the three dimensions of our management system, knowing that entropy is always a factor? There are countless stories of organizations that made great strides only to fall to the wayside. In 2001, Jim Collins wrote *Good to Great*, and then in 2009 he wrote *How the Mighty Fall*. When Jeff Liker, author of the Toyota Way series, asked Toyota's chairman what keeps him up at night, the answer was direct and immediate. The chairman answered, "That on my watch complacency will have set in." Our management system, and how we think about it, is very fragile. If we look away for only a moment, it might disappear. We must hold to it fast and pursue it endlessly.

Jim Lancaster, CEO and owner of Lantech.com LLC and author of *The Work of Management: A Daily Path to Sustainable Improvement*, likes to use the sand castle as a metaphor for this process of entropy (see Figure 7.1). You can go to the beach with your kids and spend the whole day building the most fabulous sand castle. When you come back the next day, where is

Figure 7.1 The Management System is fragile, like a sand castle

it? It's completely gone, obliterated, washed away by the tide! Our management system is as fragile as a sand castle. If we don't continuously maintain it – patting down the walls, shoring up the towers, adding water to keep it from drying out, digging out the moat – it will crumble before our eyes.

Doing daily *gemba* walks is one way of trying to see if and where performance is deteriorating, if the sand castle is crumbling and needs maintenance. Many executives don't understand why we walk around the *gemba* – it's the whole issue of entropy, to see if the system is falling apart. When Taiichi Ono visited the manufacturing *gemba* at Toyota, he stopped to check their Standard Work Forms, not so much to see how the work was supposed to be happening but to look at the revision date. If the standard had not been updated in the last six months, he knew they were getting complacent and the system was in deterioration.[2] Our management system, like a sand castle, is only as good as our ability to check continuously, to come back again and again, endlessly, to shore up its walls and towers.

Too often, when programs are not sustained, we hear management complain "the people were not committed." But leadership's role, as we discussed in Chapters 3 and 4, is just that, to bring out that commitment. Sustainment is the result of our effort to create new patterns of thinking and behaving so that "the new way" becomes "the way we've always done it." That is why deployment of the Shepherding Groups (as we saw in Chapter 5) is critical; it is one way we protect against entropy by developing habits and routines that can become part of the daily culture.

From Chaos to Complexity

If all things in the universe devolve to chaos, then what do we aspire to achieve when we want to go in the opposite direction? That is what the management system is for, to take us away from chaos and, when we get there, keep us from falling back into the abyss. Let's take a look at a more modern model of management and see how it relates to our ideas on creating and developing management systems. More specifically, let's see how our system elements of Kata and TWI engage with the forces of entropy and keep the management system from disintegrating.

---

[2] Discussion with Mr. Isao Kato in October 2018. Kato worked directly for Ono in training and development.

John Bicheno is one of the leading Lean experts in Europe, author of *The Lean Toolbox* and founder of Master's Degree programs in Lean Operations at Cardiff University in Wales and the University of Buckingham in England. At a TWI/Kata conference in Venice, Italy, in the summer of 2018, Bicheno introduced his ideas on how TWI and Kata fit into the Cynefin Framework, a powerful model that comes from systems theory and helps organizations make decisions and understand people's behavior. Cynefin (pronounced KUN-iv-in) is Welsh and means *habitat*. The theory was developed by Dave Snowden when he was working for IBM in the late 1990s.

The Cynefin Framework provides managers and leaders with a context and a perspective to better understand their observations about what is going on in their organizations so they can make better decisions for change. The model helps clarify what behaviors would work more successfully in different situations. It consists of four domains: *Simple, Complicated, Complex, Chaotic* and, at the center, *Disorder*, (see Figure 7.2). Each domain offers decision makers a framework for how best to act in a variety of situations. The two domains on the left side of the horizontal axis, *Complex* and *Chaotic*, are considered "unordered" meaning that cause-and-effect relationships can only be known after the fact, if at all.

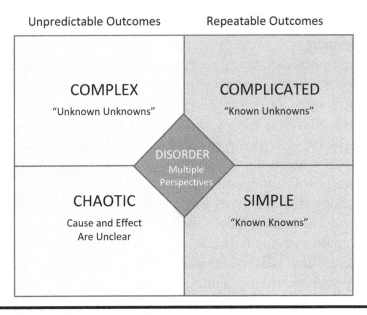

Figure 7.2   Basic Cynefin Framework

The two domains on the right side, *Complicated* and *Simple*, are considered "ordered" because cause-and-effect relationships can be identified clearly, if not always easily. The center of the framework is labeled *Disorder* and is the situation in which we simply don't know which of the four categories applies.

For a situation that falls into the *Simple* domain, where cause-and-effect relationship are clear to everyone within the organization, the "known-knowns," the best way to respond is to apply and follow the rules, the standards, or the best practices that are proven to work under the identified circumstances. The *Complicated* domain consists of the "known-unknowns" where a thorough analysis is required first to fully comprehend the cause-and-effect relationships and where there exist a range of "good" counter-measures and solutions. Here we should work rationally toward a decision using judgment and expertise rather than simply enforcing a singular rule or standard as we would in the *Simple* domain.

In the *Complex* domain, where exist the "unknown-unknowns," behavior is unpredictable, and there are no right answers that we can figure out at the moment. Since we cannot analyze the cause-and-effect relationships amongst this confusion, we must experiment to see what works and be as flexible as possible as we work our way forward to overcoming the situation. The *Chaotic* domain is characterized by crises and emergencies, and the leader's immediate job is to establish order and create stability in an effort to move the situation from chaos to complexity. The way out of the *Disorder* domain is to break down the situation into separable parts and assign each one to an appropriate domain.

As knowledge builds from our experiences responding to a particular situation, there will be a clockwise movement from *chaotic* to *complex* to *complicated* to *simple* as control is gradually gained over the situation. However, when attention wanes and entropy sets in, there will be a counter-clockwise drift as standards and practices fall to the wayside or veteran employees leave the organization to be replaced by people unfamiliar with past traditions and culture. According to the laws of entropy, situations will also tend to grow in complexity over time. In addition to this natural drift, one important insight Snowden stresses is that the *Simple* domain is actually the *danger zone* because here complacency sets in. People assume that, because conditions are stable, they will remain so indefinitely without their attention or intervention and, if action is needed, the standards and practices that worked in the past will continue doing the job. As Snowden describes it, the border between *Simple* and

Chaotic is not a line but a cliff that is easy to fall off.[3] The real danger, then, is not gravitating counter-clockwise through the domains, but going the other way, clockwise from *Simple* directly to *Chaos*. Snowden's advice is to try to stay in the *Complicated* domain and not let your organization fall into the complacency of *Simple*.[4]

Application of TWI and Kata to the Cynefin Framework

Bicheno looked at the Cynefin Framework and saw a direct correlation to places TWI and Kata can be applied in the four domains (see Figure 7.3). He saw an overlap of TWI and Kata practices being useful in the "ordered" side of the model, the right side of *Simple* and *Complicated*, where cause-and-effect relationships are known or can be found. On the "disordered" side, however, he characterized Kata by itself as being applicable in the *Complex* domain while only TWI was applicable in the *Chaotic* domain. Let's explore this to see how we can apply TWI and Kata to maintain our management system in these different realms.

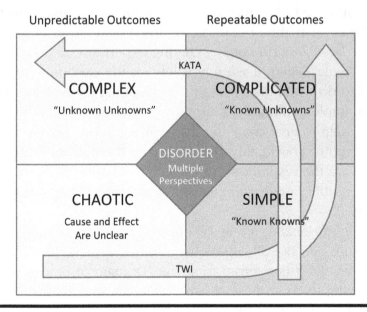

Figure 7.3   Cynefin Framework with TWI/Kata Application (by John Bicheno)

---

[3] Dave Snowden, *The Cynefin Framework* (Video: www.youtube.com/watch?v=N7oz366X0-8).
[4] Ibid.

The key to action in the *Simple* domain is to categorize a known situation and respond with a well-defined counter-measure. This is the realm of rules & regulations, standard work, and best practices where TWI certainly gives us the skills to do what we, in our organizations, know how to do best. Job Relations, in its 4-Step Method of handling people problems, takes into account the "rules and customs" that apply to the situation and guides front-line supervisors to take appropriate and effective actions that fall within the organization's "practices and policies." Job Instruction skillfully develops in people standardized work patterns based on known and quantifiable best practices. What we need to be careful to avoid is applying such straight-forward thinking and actions to problems that *were* simple in the past (and are still seen as such) but have morphed into complicated issues that cannot be solved with yesterday's practices. Kata is an effective way of avoiding this trap since we experiment with our counter-measures against obstacles that are in front of our target conditions as we PDSA our way forward. The Kata routine makes us aware of when things do not work the way we may have expected them to.

In the *Complicated* domain, because cause-and-effect relationships are not readily apparent, the action course here is to first analyze the situation to determine which of many "good" counter-measures might work. That's what makes it "complicated," because there is no one, easy answer to resolve the situation. This is the realm of experts; we need their expertise to analyze and determine the best solution course. Getting expert advice and guidance is critical, but as we've seen, if we rely solely on the experts to tell front-line people what to do while dismissing or overlooking their ideas and input, we risk failure in implementing the counter-measure itself. Here, then, is where we start with Kata to give coaching that will guide our people through the scientific method of good analysis so that they themselves can experiment their way toward the resolution. As we saw in Chapter 6, our TWI skills will prove indispensable in overcoming the many obstacles on the way to that final solution.

In the *Complex* domain, it may be impossible to identify any one "correct" counter-measure because situations here are unpredictable and, for the time being, unknowable. It is referred to as the "Domain of Emergence" because, rather than trying to control the situation, the action course is "to be patient, look for patterns, and encourage a solution to emerge."[5] This is the realm of

---

[5] MindTools website, *The Cynefin Framework: Using the Most Appropriate Problem-Solving Process* (www.mindtools.com/pages/article/cynefin-framework.htm).

innovative and creative counter-measures. Here we must conduct experiments to see what patterns emerge while accepting failure as a part of the learning process. That certainly sounds like Kata! What we learn from the results of these experiments helps us to understand the situation, little by little, and push it back to the *Complicated* domain where we can analyze and select good counter-measures.

The *Chaotic* domain is the realm of action and rapid response. Conditions here are too confusing and the risks too high to allow time for contemplative probing and analysis. The leader's role is to stop the bleeding. TWI gives supervisors specific skills to apply immediately and directly to this disorder. Job Relations directs effective action to people issues that blow up and become a "black hole," sucking all the energy out of the organization. Job Instruction quickly staunches quality, safety, and productivity issues by stabilizing work patterns around the Key Points that lock in correct and safe work. When the work procedures themselves are the source of the problem, Job Methods allows for immediate analysis of the details of the current method and acts as an "idea activator" for speedy counter-measures. Once order is established, and we begin to sense stability in the area, we move back to *Complex* where we can identify emerging patterns through experimentation that will help prevent future crises from occurring.

Keep It Complicated!

No, we are not saying in this sub-title that we should abandon the very important rule of keeping things simple. There is much profoundness in simplicity. By "complicated" here we mean (with a tinge of irony) the *Complicated* domain. But Einstein said, "If you can't explain it simply, you don't understand it well enough." He was alluding to the great effort needed to understand phenomena in their simplest terms, but that doesn't mean the phenomena are "simple." We should not "dumb down" nature. Remember, Snowden warned us that the *Simple* domain is the *danger zone* where we become complacent in our understanding of the world and make the mistake of forcing known solutions on a changing environment.[6] We are always only a few steps away from falling over the cliff into chaos.

---

[6] Perhaps that is why, more recently, he changed the name of this domain from *Simple* to *Obvious*. Just because something is obvious does not necessarily mean it is simple.

More specifically, Snowden and his colleagues cautioned managers not to oversimplify situations by forcing their solutions into the *Simple* domain. We could call this the realm of command-and-control management, where naïve managers assume they know all the answers. What the Cynefin Framework makes clear is that our business experience does not wholly exist in this one domain. Success breeds complacency, though, and we may blindly assume that we have the prescribed solution to every problem. Keep in mind that "best practices" are, by definition, also "past practices." Taiichi Ono sensed this long ago when he insisted that Standard Work at Toyota be continually updated lest workers fall into complacency. This leads to falling off the cliff from *Simple* to *Chaotic*.

Bicheno has brilliantly given us a model for understanding the uses of TWI and Kata in maintaining our management system and keeping it from devolving, through the natural effects of entropy, into chaos or perpetual complexity. Use TWI to *get out of* and *stay out of* chaos, and use Kata to gravitate from *Complex* back to *Complicated* and avoid the complacency of *Simple*. If we view the world as being a "complicated" place, then we can see how we must maintain constant vigilance and diligence in order to stay on track to getting to our goals, no matter how strong the temptation may be to fall into a sense of satisfaction with "the way things are." Our sand castle will crumble if we don't fight against the forces of nature that work to bring it down.

Management System Review[7]

The key to developing consistent patterns of ideal behavior that drive the management system is building a culture based on principles that are universal and timeless. We have endeavored to show how we have experienced building a management system that is aligned to and governed by principles. Maintaining the components we put into the system, keeping them up and running, and ensuring their alignment is perhaps the most challenging part of the mission. However, as we saw with the Shepherding Groups, much of this sustainment work is already built into the processes we have put into place. We have not neglected sustainment, leaving it until last

---

[7] We are greatly indebted to the cooperation and help of Paul Terry in helping us develop this review process. Paul has had a long career with O.C. Tanner and is one of one of six members of the Shingo Examiners Committee for the Shingo Prize.

when all the other work has been done. Sustainment is an integrated part of the meta-processes we are practicing, and these meta-patterns, by definition, are meant to build and enforce change in culture that is self-sustaining through meta-patterns' pervasive and repetitive structure.

There is still a vital piece that cannot be ignored. Why do you go to the doctor for an annual check-up? Why pay a visit to the dentist every six months, even when you don't have a toothache? Why bring your car to the service center or dealer every 3,000 miles, or maybe more for newer models, when it's running fine? The answer, of course, is to check to see whether everything is going well with your body by taking blood tests, making sure you don't have any new cavities by looking at x-rays, and ensuring your engine is running well by changing the oil and taking a look under the hood. When you go into a check-up with your doctor, she may ask you very casually, as Patrick's doctor does, "So what's going on?" It's an open-ended question. The doctor listens carefully, without interruption and with an open mind, to assess the patient's current condition. That's the start. After some basic checks – vital signs, listening to your heart and breathing, feeling your tummy, checking your reflexes, etc. – she will give you suggestions of what to do going forward to correct any issues and to stay healthy.

The final piece to locking in the management system, we have found, is to set up and run a regular Management System Review, just like an annual physical check-up, of each facility to examine its culture and identify behaviors and shifting patterns of work at all levels to see if they consistently reflect ideal behaviors, meta-patterns, needed to create a sustainable culture of operational excellence. We hesitate to call these "assessments" since the purpose is not to pass a test or get a score. On the contrary, a review should be a motivating learning experience for the local entity that gives the people in the organization a good sense of where they are at in their management system development and where they need to go and why. While bringing out and honoring the pieces they have been able to improve, it should also help them identify gaps in their execution and give guidance on how to close them. The review should capture the overall maturity the facility has achieved with the management system and deliver a "reality check" at that moment in time.

Just as we developed the skills and responsibilities of Shepherds in the Shepherding Groups, we must select a diverse team of assessors who are coached on how to do the reviews. These assessors can come from various areas and disciplines in the organization with the rule that they will never assess their own department, only others. They must have a positive and respectful attitude of service that encourages development of the management system in others. Most importantly, they must be ambassadors of the management system living and radiating the guiding principles of the organization.

These assessors will periodically go to other departments in the organization, or even to other facilities if the organization has that kind of scale, and assess the degree to which the management system principles are evident in the behavior of every employee. Assessors observe actions and determine the frequency, duration, intensity, and scope of the desired principle-based behaviors. They observe the degree to which leaders in the organization focus on principles and culture, as well as whether managers focus on aligning systems to drive ideal behaviors at all levels. Again, the review is not to "audit" compliance to the system, but to look for evidence that the culture is adapting and evolving in the direction we want it to develop. The focus is to determine whether the facility is fundamentally improving for the long term rather than just going through the motions of another "flavor-of-the-month" initiative.

In order to aid in these reviews, long lists of analytical questions should be prepared ahead of time so that assessors can use them to drive interviews with employees at three levels – top leadership, line management, and front-line employees – to help them determine the degree to which ideal principle-based behaviors have been embedded in the management system culture. These questions should be open ended so that they do *not* elicit simple "yes" and "no" answers. On the other hand, they should be designed to bring out thoughtful responses with the purpose of getting people to "show" their thinking and explain the How and the Why of their engagement with the management system. The assessors are not there to "get into the weeds" of the tactics and details of what is being done, because the people in each area own that tactical approach. The questions are solely aimed at better understanding the thinking and behavior that demonstrates attachment to the guiding principles.

The assessors do not need to ask all the questions on the list; they should follow their own impressions of where the dialogue in each interview is going and explore areas that better lead them to understanding the true state of the management system at that level in that part of the organization. While you need to develop your own set of questions based on the management system you are aspiring to develop, for reference on how to write and organize them, Appendix 1 contains questions we use to review the overall management system and its alignment to the three dimensions of Purpose,

People, and Process. Appendix 2 is a list of questions directed at TWI implementation, and Appendix 3 shows a list of questions directed at Kata deployment.

Finally, assessors should take the results of their interviews and observations and prepare a feedback report that highlights the strengths and opportunities they found. We feel that these reports can be skillfully written to highlight the guiding principles, to couch the feedback and guidance within the context of the principles so that, even in these reviews, we continue driving the principle of *Constancy of Purpose*. The review report will be a catalyst for people to recommit to these principles as they see, from the feedback, how their efforts help and can continue contributing to a management system under which everyone thrives.

This is an actual report we made for a hospital when reviewing TWI activity. For brevity, we condensed it to selected comments that are representative of the kind of feedback that seeks to be encouraging and motivating.

TWI REVIEW FEEDBACK REPORT

November 5, 2018

1. PEOPLE

Strengths

- JR across the board is becoming a part of the culture, language, and how you treat each other on a regular basis.
- Including people in JM projects who are not involved in other management system activities and "giving them a voice," is a good demonstration of **Respect Every Individual**.
- There is a clear vision of how consistency of leadership and using JR as a standard practice is a benefit to the entire facility.

Opportunities

- In order to **Lead with Humility**, you may want to consider reengaging with JI on a much narrower level which is connected to a strategic gap (e.g. rolling out JI only in the ICU to combat CAUDI). How would you do that?

– Recognizing the fact that everyone is too busy to apply JI, use the principle of **Respect Every Individual** to better understand people's position while working together with them to find a way to get training up and running.
– In the follow-up JR sessions, how could you think more about encouraging use of the Foundations to build stronger relations that prevent problems from happening?

2. PROCESS
Strengths

– By bringing diverse people together to practice JM, you are applying the principle of **Seek Perfection** by breaking down silo-thinking and making the best use of each employee's ideas and creativity in a collaborative effort.
– There was a good example of following up on a quality problem, an uptick in CLABSIs, by discovering a falloff in training quality. Retraining was performed and the problem corrected showing a strong **Focus on Process**.

Opportunities

– As you gain experience using JM, you can use it more extensively in order to **Focus on Process** by connecting JM activities to strategic initiatives and using it more proactively in Kata and Idea Generation activities.
– Consider reengaging with the JI process, identifying priorities for training with available trainers, bolstering the overall trainer group, and developing meaningful training schedules to strengthen the training process? This would **Assure Quality at the Source**.

3. PURPOSE
Strengths

– Follow-up on JR (e.g. surveys) is being carried out throughout the organization. This will provide the foundation, through strong relations, for JI and JM to be fully integrated into the management system, following the principle of **Think Systemically**.

– You have a clear concept of using TWI as a "bridge" connecting strategy deployment with Kata practice and usage of the A3 tool. This is a clear application of the principles of **Think Systemically** and **Constancy of Purpose**.

Opportunities

– JI is not connected to strategic initiatives and therefore there is no **Constancy of Purpose**. The initial roll out of making people use JI where it wasn't needed shows the importance of this principle. But even with multiple success examples, there is no momentum to recreating these successes. And in these success examples, there is no way to guarantee the next person coming on line gets trained correctly.
– How can you develop a better vision to connect both JI and JM with strategic objectives in order to better **Think Systemically**?

4. RESULTS

Strengths

– There were consistent expressions acknowledging the importance of caring for patients and it is clear all employees are passionate about **Create Value for Customer**.
– Where poor results were found, you were able to reengage and correct the problems.

Opportunities

– Front line leaders must "connect the dots" across all areas listed in the Safe Room on the strategic A3s cascading through tactical A3s to find results at the lowest levels of the organization in order to close gaps.
– Find ways to validate that you are training the correct JI way and verify if the work methods trained are being performed correctly and being sustained.

Conclusion – Getting Back to Principles

This chapter has looked at how we consolidate all our efforts around creating an effective management system while fighting the natural tendency of all things to degrade and disintegrate. While this is a never-ending evolutionary development process, and we are always, always somewhere far short of where we wanted or expected to be at any given time, we have found that looking for evidence of our guiding principles being embedded into the culture is the "touchpoint" where we can effectively engage the workforce in a lively and upbeat dialogue on how we are doing with the management system. This brings us back full circle, then, to the very beginning, where we started, seeking to create a management system that embodies the guiding principles we wanted to live by in order to prosper and succeed. The principles guide and direct the management system, and the management system lays fertile ground for the principles to grow and prosper. In the end, if we have nudged the culture and started it rolling down that gradual slope toward a principle-based environment, then we succeeded with our management system. Don't look at the scoreboard; just follow the process.

Appendix 1: Overall Management System Review Questions[1]

Part 1 People

Questions for Leaders (key questions are in bold):

1. **Please tell me how you are incorporating the 10 Guiding Principles of operational excellence into your own life and your personal efforts to reinforce these principles as a part of the management system culture.**
   a. **How often do you reflect on your progress? Why is that a valuable practice?**
   b. **How often do you ask for feedback from those you work with regarding how you are doing with this challenge?**
2. **How do you ensure that your people understand the expectation to practice the 10 Guiding Principles every day? Why is that important?**
3. **How are the 10 Guiding Principles connected to organization strategy?**
4. **Explain how you hold people accountable.**
   a. **Please describe your system of outlining and following up on expectations.**

---

[1] This Appendix developed and written by Paul Terry.

5. **Describe your organization's problem solving/improvement process, including the role of teams.**
6. **Please explain how committed you are to the practice of empowering people at all levels to own their processes and drive improvements. Why is that important?**
7. **Show me your leader standard work. How do you lead from the *gemba*, the actual place where work is done?**
8. **How are you moving away from a style of command-and-control management? Why is this important?**
9. Describe how you help leaders, managers, and associates develop effective communication, listening, and relationship-building skills.
10. How do you teach problem-solving skills to your people?
11. List efforts being used to achieve a high level of employee engagement.
12. Describe how you utilize the practice of asking open-ended questions. Why is that important?
13. How is escalation protocol used in your organization?
14. How do you encourage people at all levels to help define and identify ideal, principle-based behaviors? Why is that important?
15. How often do you spend time alongside associates, at locations where the actual work is performed, listening to and learning from the people? Why is that important?
16. Please provide examples of when you have sought and listened to input from others. Also, relate examples of when you have acted on their input.
17. When was the last time you publicly acknowledged insights that you have gained from others?
18. How do you ensure that you have a safe environment, that the safety of all associates is perceived as the highest priority?
19. How do you ensure that people have the information they need to be successful in their work?
    a. Describe how open and effective you are at communicating with people at all levels and all shifts so that they feel respected and cared about.
20. How does Policy Deployment connect the long-term vision and mission of the organization with teams directly serving customers?
21. Explain how the voice of the customer drives Policy Deployment.
22. How engaged would you say people are in huddles (e.g., the daily safety huddle)? What leads you to that conclusion?
23. Explain how and why you do rounding with your managers. Who is involved?

24. Tell me about the coaching system you practice here.
    a. How often do you have face-to-face, one-on-one coaching with your direct reports?
    b. How do you provide feedback to managers regarding their skills and competencies?
    c. How often do you update development plans for your managers, in support of their training needs and career objectives?
    d. How do you teach coaching skills to your leaders and managers?
25. Please explain your leadership development philosophy and program.
26. How often do you update your succession plans?
27. How do you benchmark other entities within the organization's group or organizations outside of the group to identify best practices?
28. How do you share best practices with other entities?
29. Is there anything else that you want to share with me?

Questions for Managers (key questions are in bold):

1. **Please tell me how you are incorporating the 10 Guiding Principles of operational excellence into your own life and your personal efforts to reinforce these principles as a part of the management system culture.**
    a. **How often do you reflect on your progress? Why is that important?**
    b. **How often do you ask for feedback from those you work with regarding how you are doing with this challenge?**
2. **How do you ensure that your people understand the expectation to practice the 10 Guiding Principles every day?**
3. **How are the 10 Guiding Principles connected to organization strategy?**
4. **Explain how you hold people accountable.**
    a. **Please describe your system of outlining and following up on expectations.**
5. **Describe your organization's problem solving/improvement process, including the role of teams.**
6. **How do you make sure that decision making is enabled at the appropriate level in your area, empowering people to own and manage their processes?**
7. **What is the reaction by leaders when a mistake happens?**

    a. **How much is there a focus on fixing the process versus disciplining a person?**

8. **Please provide examples of when you have sought and listened to the input from others.**

    a. **Relate examples of when you have acted on their input.**

9. **How do you ensure that your people have the information they need to be successful in their work?**

    a. **How open and effective are you at communicating with people on all levels and all shifts, so that they feel respected and cared about?**

10. Describe how you help your associates develop effective communication, listening, and relationship-building skills.

11. How much time do you spend each day with your people where the actual work is performed, listening to and learning from them? Why is this important?

12. Explain how you do rounding with your people.

13. How often do you have face-to-face coaching with each of your direct reports? Why is this important?

14. How do you encourage your people to help define and identify ideal, principle-based behaviors? Why is that important?

15. When was the last time that you publicly acknowledged insights that you have gained from others?

    a. Please relate that experience.

16. Explain how you coach and mentor your people to follow standard work in the execution of principle-based systems. Why is this important?

17. Describe your approach for developing the talents and capabilities of your people.

    a. How often do you create/update development plans for your associates, in support of their training needs and career objectives?

    b. How do you provide feedback to associates regarding their skills and competencies?

18. How do you ensure that you have a safe environment, that the safety of all associates and patients is perceived as the highest priority?

19. How do you know that your direct reports and associates look at the information on the boards?

    a. Is it helpful and useful to them?

    b. Do they understand what is on the boards?

   c. How do you make sure that the information on the boards is up to date?
   d. How often is the information discussed in huddles?
20. How well organized are your work units/areas regarding storage and a proper place for everything? What benefits could come from being well organized?
   a. Possible answers: Identify and reduce waste (e.g., save time, increase safety)
21. Is there anything else that you want to share with me?

Questions for Associates (key questions are in bold):

1. **Is this a great place to work?**
   a. **Why are you here instead of somewhere else?**
2. **Please tell me how you are incorporating the 10 Guiding Principles of operational excellence into your own life and your personal efforts to reinforce these principles as a part of the management system culture.**
   a. **How often do you reflect on your progress? Why is this important?**
   b. **How often do you ask for feedback from those you work with regarding how you are doing with this challenge?**
3. **How are the 10 Guiding Principles connected to organization strategy?**
4. **Describe your organization's problem solving/improvement process, including the role of teams.**
5. **Do you feel that your leader knows you and cares about you?**
   a. **Why do you say that?**
6. **Do you trust your leaders? Why?**
7. **What is the overall vision and mission of the organization?**
8. **Please provide examples of when leaders have sought and listened to your input.**
   a. **Relate examples of when they have acted on your input.**
9. **Can you give me examples of how you are empowered to make decisions and improvements relative to your processes? Why is this important?**
10. **Do you feel respected by leaders and co-workers?**
   a. **Why do you feel that way?**
11. Do leaders adhere to the 10 Guiding Principles during rough times?

12. Do you view your leaders as servant leaders?
    a. Why do you feel that way?
13. Please give me some examples of how you look for and acknowledge ideal, principle-based behaviors in the actions of co-workers. Why is this important?
14. How do you show commitment to the organization's policies and the 10 Guiding Principles that you are expected to embrace?
15. How often do you see your manager or senior leaders where the actual work is performed? Why is this important?
16. How good do you think this organization is at being willing to let associates implement ideas coming from the people closest to the work?
17. How do you ensure that you have a safe environment, that the safety of all associates and patients is perceived as the highest priority?
    a. Is safety discussed in every meeting? Why is that important?
18. How do you demonstrate respect for co-workers?
19. How do you reach out to others in the organization to learn from them, including leaders, managers, and peers? Why is this important?
20. How are you reaching out to share personal learnings and insights with co-workers? Why is this important?
21. What are you doing to make yourself more valuable to the organization, taking personal responsibility for your own personal development?
22. Do you feel that you have opportunities to develop your talents and capabilities, based on your career objectives? Why do you say that?
23. What is the reaction by leaders when a mistake happens?
    a. Is there a focus on fixing the process or on disciplining a person?
24. How well organized are your work units/areas regarding storage and a proper place for everything? What benefits could come from being well organized?
    a. Possible answers: Identify and reduce waste (e.g., save time, increase safety)
25. Is there anything else that you want to share with me?

Part 2 Process (Continuous Improvement)

Questions for Leaders (key questions are in bold):

1. **Please describe your system for Continuous Process Improvement?**
   a. **How does it connect to Policy Deployment?**

2. **What do you do to ensure that the principles of Continuous Improvement are deeply embedded into the mindset of every person in the organization, in all areas and at all levels?**
   a. **How much of your time do you spend focusing on this?**
3. **How have you incorporated Continuous Improvement efforts into your daily leader standard work? Why is that important?**
4. **Do you believe in the philosophy that "Improving the work IS the work"?**
   a. **How have you incorporated that philosophy into your job? Why is that important?**
5. **Please tell me about the last time you recognized managers or associates for demonstrating ideal principle-based behavior or for achieving business goals.**
6. **How are improvement initiatives and projects prioritized and selected?**
7. **Please tell me about the last Continuous Improvement initiative you were involved in.**
8. **Please tell me about the Continuous Improvement initiative you are involved in now.**
9. **How do you feel about the emphasis here in identifying waste reduction opportunities?**
   a. **What are the 8 forms of waste?**
   b. **Please give me some examples of how you have been able to "see" and eliminate waste.**
   c. **What are your thoughts on implementing an 8 Waste Certification Program?**
   d. **How does silo mentality limit our ability to think systemically and to fully utilize the skills and abilities of others?**
      i. **What are you doing to break down barriers between departments so that efforts to collaborate through multidisciplinary teams are more effective?**
10. Explain how you have established personal accountability to others for your Continuous Improvement efforts.
11. Tell me how you celebrate accomplishments with your people before setting goals to move on to the next level. Why is this important?
12. How do you encourage the setting of stretch goals in all areas to challenge managers and associates to continually raise the bar on performance?

    a. How do you support and encourage your managers to improve systems and processes when results are less than expected?

13. How do you encourage your people to select and apply the appropriate tools to understand root cause prior to implementing countermeasures? Why is this important?

14. How often do you participate with managers and associates on improvement initiatives, as required? Why is this important?

15. How many improvement ideas is each associate expected to generate in a year?
    a. What percentage of your people meet that expectation?
    b. How many implemented suggestions did your people generate last year? How many people generated at least one implemented idea?

16. How do you teach your associates that they are expected to stop a procedure or a process that is being performed incorrectly, even if someone else is performing the procedure? Why is that important?

17. What is the role of the Shepherding Groups in the organization's Management System? How do they add value?

18. Explain the importance of the daily Safety Huddle.

19. What is the process for making sure that all goals are measurable?

20. How and where are strategic A3s visually displayed? How often and to whom is progress reported?

21. How and where are tactical A3s visually displayed? How often and to whom is progress reported?

22. How does consistently following standard work make it possible for your people to see abnormalities?
    a. What is your process for dealing with abnormalities?

23. What is the role of associates in Continuous Improvement, and how are skills related to improvement and teamwork included in job requirements?

24. Describe efforts to identify and eliminate all forms of waste in all areas.

25. What are you doing to eliminate all forms of overburdening your people?

26. How do you partner with your suppliers to minimize total cost to your value stream?

27. How does the concept of listening to the voice of the customer apply?

28. Please explain how the concept of flowing and pulling value is based on the cadence of real customer demand.
    a. How have you utilized Kanbans to facilitate flow and pull?

29. Tell me about your efforts to improve department layouts to optimize flow.

30. Explain to me what you are doing to improve OEE (Operational Equipment Efficiency).
31. Is there anything else you want to share with me?

Questions for Managers (key questions are in bold):

1. **How would you describe your system for Continuous Process Improvement?**
2. **How have you incorporated Continuous Improvement efforts into your daily leader standard work? Why?**
3. **Explain how you give constant feedback and encouragement to your people to follow standard work and to look for ways to improve their processes. Why is this important?**
4. **What do you do to ensure that the principles of Continuous Improvement are deeply embedded into the mindset of every person in your area?**
   a. **How much of your time do you spend focusing on eliminating waste or increasing value to the customer?**
5. **Do you believe in the philosophy that "Improving the work IS the work"? How have you incorporated that philosophy into your job? Why is this important?**
6. **What is the process for making sure that all goals are measurable?**
7. **Please tell me about the last time that you recognized your people for demonstrating ideal principle-based behavior or for achieving business goals.**
8. **Please tell me about the last Continuous Improvement initiative you were involved in.**
9. **Please tell me about the Continuous Improvement initiative you are involved in now.**
10. **How do you feel about the emphasis here in identifying waste reduction opportunities?**
    a. **What are the 8 forms of waste?**
    b. **Please give me some examples of how you have been able to "see" and eliminate waste.**
    c. **How does silo mentality limit our ability to think systemically and to fully utilize the skills and abilities of others?**
       i. **What are you doing to break down barriers between departments so that efforts to collaborate with others outside of your immediate discipline are more effective?**

11. Explain how you have established personal accountability to others for your Continuous Improvement efforts. Why is this important?
12. Describe efforts to identify and eliminate all forms of waste in your area.
13. What are you doing to eliminate all forms of overburdening your people?
14. How do you partner with your suppliers to minimize total cost to your value stream?
15. Please show me some examples of how you have mistake-proofed some processes.
16. Please tell me about your efforts to improve department layouts to optimize flow.
17. Explain to me what you are doing to improve OEE (Operational Equipment Efficiency).
18. How do you go about encouraging the setting of stretch goals in all areas to challenge associates to continually raise the bar on performance?
    a. How do you support and encourage your people to improve processes when results are less than expected?
19. Tell me how you celebrate accomplishments with your people before setting goals to move on to the next level. Why is this important?
20. How are improvement initiatives prioritized and selected?
21. How deep is your understanding of the tools to identify and prioritize gaps and to understand root cause prior to implementing countermeasures?
    a. For example, Pareto, 5-Whys, Root Cause Analysis, Fishbone, Spaghetti, Process Maps, Value Stream Maps, Error-Proofing, Visual Management, 5S, 8 Wastes, Abnormality Tracking/Focus, etc.
22. How do you encourage and train your people to select and apply the appropriate tools to understand root cause prior to implementing countermeasures? Why is this important?
23. How are value stream maps used to understand flow and to challenge the value of each step, looking for waste-elimination opportunities?
24. How often do you participate with associates as required on improvement initiatives? Why is this important?
25. How do you emphasize with your associates that they are expected to stop a procedure or a process that is being performed incorrectly, even if someone else is performing the procedure?
    a. If that were to happen, how do you ensure that the error does not reoccur?

26. Please share with me your supplier development strategy and current initiatives.
27. How many of your processes have defined standard work?
    a. How do you verify that standard work is being followed?
28. How does consistently following standard work make it possible for your people to see abnormalities?
    a. What is your process for dealing with abnormalities?
29. How many improvement ideas is each associate expected to generate in a year?
    a. What percentage of your people meet that expectation?
    b. How many implemented suggestions did your people generate last year?
    c. How many people generated at least one implemented idea?
30. Is there anything else you want to share with me?

Questions for Associates (key questions are in bold):

1. **Please describe the system for Continuous Process Improvement?**
2. **Do you believe in the philosophy that "Improving the work IS the work," that when the philosophy of improvement is integrated with work, each person accepts responsibility for improvement?**
   a. **Why is this important?**
   b. **How have you incorporated that philosophy into your job?**
3. **How much time do you spend daily focusing on Continuous Improvement to eliminate waste or to increase value to the customer? Why is that important?**
4. **Please tell me about the last Continuous Improvement initiative you were involved in.**
5. **Please tell me about the Continuous Improvement initiative you are involved in now.**
6. **If you could change one thing, what would it be?**
   a. **What is preventing you from changing it now?**
7. **Is standard work important? Why?**
8. **How do you feel about the emphasis here in identifying waste reduction opportunities?**
   a. **What are the 8 forms of waste?**
   b. **Please give me some examples of how you have been able to "see" and eliminate waste.**

    c. **How does silo mentality limit our ability to think systemically and to fully utilize the skills and abilities of others?**
      i. **What are you doing to break down barriers between departments so that efforts to collaborate with others outside of your immediate discipline are more effective?**

9. How far has your organization come in ensuring that the principles of Continuous Improvement are deeply embedded into the mindset of every person?

10. What opportunities exist here to reduce the distance that you walk each day?

11. Which improvement initiatives currently being worked on in your area are related to customer feedback?

12. Have you participated in idea generation? Tell me about your experience with that tool.
    a. Is it a good tool? Why do you say that?

13. Who determines what projects or improvements are to be worked on in your area?

14. Tell me about the different tools that you understand and feel capable of using to drive improvement initiatives.

15. How do you select and apply the appropriate tools of Continuous Improvement to understand root cause prior to implementing countermeasures?

16. How well do you understand the principles (the why) behind the tools (the how)? Please explain.

17. Please tell me about the last time that you were recognized for demonstrating ideal principle-based behavior or for achieving business goals. Who gave you the recognition?

18. Have you ever stopped a procedure or a process that was not correct, even if someone else was performing the procedure? Please explain.

19. How well do you understand the standard work (work instructions) for the processes that you perform?
    a. Where can you find standard work documentation for the processes that you perform?

20. How often do you refer to work instructions to verify that you are following them correctly?

21. When was the last time that you suggested a change to a standard work procedure?

22. How does consistently following standard work make it possible for you to see abnormalities?

a. What is your process for dealing with abnormalities?
23. How many of your processes have defined standard work?
    a. How do you verify that standard work is being followed?
24. Describe all efforts to identify and eliminate all forms of waste in your area.
25. Please show me some examples of how you have mistake-proofed some processes.
26. Is there anything else you want to share with me?

Part 3 Purpose (Alignment)

Questions for Leaders (key questions are in bold):

1. **Please describe your overall strategy deployment process.**
2. **How do you ensure that your managers and associates understand their connection to overall, high-level strategies? Why is that important?**
3. **How often do you talk as leaders about a common, clear, and compelling vision of the future? Why is that important?**
   a. **How often do you discuss your vision of the future with managers and associates?**
4. **Please explain your system of cascading "catch ball" as it relates to your Policy Deployment process.**
   a. **Why is cascading catch ball in all areas of the organization an important tool of alignment?**
5. **How often do you hear "us vs. them" language here? Please explain.**
6. **How are decisions made regarding which projects or priorities should be worked on first or next?**
   a. **Why is that an important question relative to the concept of alignment?**
7. **Why is leader standard work an important concept relative to alignment?**
   a. **Show me your personal leader standard work.**
8. How do you set strategic objectives for the organization, consistent with corporate directives?
   a. Explain how you have improved that process over the past few years.
9. How do you encourage your managers better align their systems to drive ideal, principle-based behaviors? Why is that important?

10. How do you utilize the concept of tiered meetings to drive strategy deployment?
11. What methods of communication exist to ensure that your message is spread consistently across the organization to people on all shifts and in all areas? Why is communication important as a vehicle for alignment?
12. Explain how your communication system provides for the flow on information both up and down the organization. Why is that important?
    a. What is your system for analyzing feedback information that flows up to leadership?
13. Explain how information is easily accessible and usable across the extended enterprise.
14. How important are huddle boards as a tool to communicate constancy of purpose?
15. What are the constant features on your huddle boards across all areas of the organization? Why is that important?
16. Explain why the things on the board are "the right things."
17. Explain how key metrics are simply displayed and visible in all areas.
18. How do you know that people understand what they see on the boards?
19. Explain the concept of rounding and how you employ it across the organization.
    a. What is the expectation of leaders relative to rounding?
    b. What benefits do you realize from that effort?
    c. How does the practice of rounding relate to the concept of "go and see?"
20. Explain to me the importance of accountability in the organization. Why is it important?
    a. How do you ensure accountability at all levels?
21. Why is it important to share with managers and associates an understanding of strategy, tactics, and metrics and how their work connects with the big picture? Describe your system for ensuring that happens.
22. What do you do to remind managers of the systemic implications of things that you discuss as leaders? Why is that important?
23. How do you ensure that the voice of the customer is clearly heard across the entire organization? Why is that important?
24. How are support functions such as IT, Finance, and HR seamlessly integrated to help drive value creation?

25. Please give me some example of how you find opportunities for the organization to give back to the community and how you encourage others to support those opportunities.
26. Is there anything else you want to share with me?

Questions for Managers (key questions are in bold):

1. **How do you ensure that your people understand their connection to overall, high-level strategies? Why is that important?**
2. **Please explain your system of cascading "catch ball" as it relates to your Policy Deployment process. Why is catch ball important as a tool of alignment?**
3. **How are decisions made regarding which projects or priorities should be worked on first or next?**
   a. **Why is that an important question relative to the concept of alignment?**
4. **Explain the concept of rounding and how you employ it in your area.**
   a. **What is the expectation of leaders relative to rounding?**
   b. **What benefits do you realize from that effort?**
5. **How often do you hear "us vs. them" language here? Please explain.**
6. **Why is leader standard work an important concept relative to alignment?**
   a. **Show me your personal leader standard work.**
7. How do you work to better align your management systems to drive ideal, principle-based behaviors? Why is that important?
8. Explain to me the importance of accountability in the organization. Why is it important?
   a. How do you ensure accountability at all levels?
9. How often do you talk about a common, clear, and compelling vision of the future? Why is that important?
10. How often do you discuss your vision of the future with your people? Why is that important?
11. How important are huddle boards as a tool to communicate constancy of purpose?
12. What are the constant features on your huddle boards across all areas of the organization? Why is that important?

13. How do you know that your people understand what is on the board?
14. Explain how key metrics are simply displayed and visible in all areas.
15. What methods of communication exist to ensure that your message is spread consistently across the organization to people on all shifts and in all areas?
    a. Why is communication important as a vehicle for alignment?
16. Do you feel that you have the information that you need to be effective in your work? Why is that important?
17. How are your huddles and team meetings opportunities to not only share information, but to also discuss ideas and suggestions for improvement?
    a. How often do you discuss versus just share?
18. How effective are your meetings in fostering discussion and expanding thinking beyond your own area?
19. Why is it important to share with associates an understanding of strategy, tactics, and metrics and how their work connects with the big picture?
    a. Describe your system for ensuring that happens.
20. What do you do to remind your people about the systemic implications of things that you discuss with them? Why is that important?
21. How do you ensure that the voice of the customer is clearly heard by the associates in your area? Why is that important?
22. How do you share improvements or ideas across the organization to other areas and other shifts?
23. Please give me some example of how you find opportunities in your area to give back to the community and how you encourage your people to support those opportunities.
24. Is there anything else you want to share with me?

Questions for Associates (key questions are in bold):

1. **How do your efforts and projects connect to overall, high-level strategies? Why is that important?**
2. **Please explain your system of cascading "catch ball" as it relates to your Policy Deployment process.**
    a. **Why is catch ball important as a tool of alignment?**
3. **How are decisions made regarding which projects or priorities should be worked on first or next?**

    a. **Why is that an important question relative to the concept of alignment?**
4. **How effective is executive leadership and your manager in communicating across the organization?**
    a. **How do all associates on all shifts get information consistently and in a timely manner?**
5. **How often do you hear "us vs. them" language here? Please explain.**
6. **What does the board mean to you? What on the board do you look at and find helpful?**
7. How often do you talk with your manager about a common, clear, and compelling vision of the future? Why is it important to have those discussions?
8. Do you feel that you have the information that you need to be effective in your work? Why is that important?
9. What performance and behavioral metrics do you discuss in your huddles?
    a. Why are those metrics important to you and the organization?
10. How are your huddles and team meetings used as opportunities to not only share information, but to also discuss ideas and suggestions for improvement?
11. How effective are your meetings in fostering discussion and expanding thinking beyond your own area?
12. How often do you have opportunities to learn about other areas in the organization?
    a. Do you ever flex into other areas? Why is that important?
13. Please give me some example of how you support the organization in giving back to the community.
14. Is there anything else you want to share with me?

Part 4 Results

Questions for Leaders (key questions are in bold):

1. **Explain how you, as leaders, have identified the essential key metrics to report on.**
    a. **How have you made the reporting of those metrics simple and consistent across the organization? Why is that important?**

2. **How do you focus on both KPI results (lag metrics) and KBI behaviors (lead metrics) with an emphasis on identifying the proactive behavioral lead metrics that will drive lag results metric? Why is that important?**
3. **Please explain the lead metric (KBI behavior) associated with each lag KPI metric.**
4. **Please share the results from customer and employee feedback surveys.**
   a. **What are you doing to improve those scores?**
5. How do you ensure that performance measures drive the right behaviors?
6. Please explain your company scorecard to me.
7. How is the voice of the customer represented on your scorecard? Why is that important?
8. Describe your system for discussing business results with employees.
   a. How do you give them the opportunity to ask and receive answers to questions? Why is that important?
9. How do you measure your market share?

Questions for Managers (key questions are in bold):

1. **How do you focus the attention of your people on both KPI results (lag metrics) and KBI behaviors (lead metrics) with an emphasis on identifying the proactive behavioral lead metrics that will drive lag results metric? Why is that important?**
2. **Describe your system for discussing business results with employees.**
   a. **Do you give employees the opportunity to ask and receive answers to questions? Why is that important?**
3. **Please explain your company scorecard to me.**
4. **Describe your systems for placing value creation and waste elimination at the heart of management and improvement efforts.**
   a. **Why is it important for your people to clearly understand those systems?**
5. How often do you discuss with your people the systems and principles that are creating actual results? Why is that important?
6. How is the voice of the customer represented on your scorecard? Why is that important?

Questions for Associates (key questions are in bold):

1. **Explain the relationship between lead and lag metrics.**
   a. **Which do you focus on as the proactive driver of end results?**
   b. **What is the connection between what you do each day and the end results you achieve?**
2. **How often do you receive regular updates regarding overall business results for the organization, with the opportunity to ask questions? Why is that important?**
3. **How do results metrics help you prioritize improvement efforts that will impact the areas where improvement is most needed? Why is that important?**
4. **How do you know if you are winning today?**
   a. **What visual signals do you look at each day to know where you stand?**
   b. **If you are not winning today, what can you do right now to make today a success?**
5. How often do you discuss with your manager actual results and the systems and principles that are creating those results? Why is that important?
6. How do you identify and consider the voice of the customer in your improvement plans? Why is that important?

Appendix 2: TWI Implementation Review Questions

Part 1 TWI Training Overall

Questions for Leaders (key questions are in bold):

1. **What does TWI mean to this organization? What would you say is TWI's role in promoting the principles to which the organization aspires?**
2. How does your organization support the training and application of the TWI skills? What is your role in that support?
3. How integral are the TWI skills to achieving the goals and objectives toward which the organization is working?
4. Explain your process of managing trainers of the 10-hour class and if they are doing an effective job.
5. Where do you want to be a year from now with TWI overall?

Questions for Managers (key questions are in bold):

1. **Describe the utilization of the TWI methods and how they are applied on a regular (daily) basis?**
   a. **How does their application help you achieve your managerial responsibilities?**
2. How are the different elements of the TWI methodologies used by your organization and your department specifically?
   a. What do they mean to you as a manager?
3. Please show me a plan for your TWI strategy.

Questions for Associates (key questions are in bold):

1. **What value does TWI provide you in your day-to-day activities?**
2. **Please show me an example.**

Part 2 Job Instruction

Questions for Leaders (key questions are in bold):

1. **What is the coverage of Job Instruction trainers you have developed in your organization (e.g., ratio of trainers to staff)?**
   a. **How does that training capacity assist in achieving the organization's goals?**
   b. **How active are the Job Instruction trainers, and why is it critical to maintain this instruction ability?**
2. **Describe how the organization validates these trainers to ensure they are teaching jobs properly using the JI 4-step method.**
   a. **What happens if they are not?**
3. **How do you think about and implement a verification process for Job Instruction to ensure learners are following the processes they were taught?**
   a. **Describe your process for ensuring that learners are following the processes they were taught.**
4. Describe how the organization decides which tasks and duties are selected to be trained using Job Instruction, or is training done on an "as needed" basis?
   a. How does this process align job instruction with the organization's objectives?
   b. Please give an example of how that worked.
5. Describe the role Job Instruction plays in your organization on employee factors such as motivation, retention, engagement, and empowerment.
   a. Please give some examples.
6. What is the process for keeping Job Instruction Breakdowns up to date, and how do you manage the training after a JIB has been updated?
7. How do you measure the effectiveness of Job Instruction in your organization?
8. Where do you want to be with Job Instruction a year from now?

Questions for Managers (key questions are in bold):

1. **Describe the role Job Instruction plays as a regular part of how work content and quality are managed and improved in your department.**
2. **Describe how Job Instruction is used to achieve organizational objectives.**
   a. **Please give some examples of when and how this has happened.**
3. **Please describe a situation when Job Instruction was used as a remedy for handling a performance problem.**
   a. **What were the results?**
4. What are your thoughts on standardizing the way everyone does work in the organization?
   a. What benefits would that give?
   b. How does Job Instruction help with that standardization?
5. Has using the Job Instruction method for training people improved your relationships with the people you trained?
   a. If so, in what way?
6. What obstacles do you face when using Job Instruction to achieve your organizational goals?
   a. Describe how you were able to overcome those obstacles.
7. Please demonstrate teaching a job using the Job Instruction method.
8. How do you think about and use the Training Timetable?
   a. Can you show an example?
9. Please describe any actions around Job Instruction that have emanated from your Safety Huddle or Kata Coaching activities.

Questions for Associates (key questions are in bold):

1. **Have you ever been taught to perform a task or function by a TWI trainer using the Job Instruction method?**
   a. **If so, please describe the process and what it meant to you.**
2. What jobs have you been taught using the Job Instruction method?
   a. Do you know why you were taught those jobs?
   b. If so, why?

3. What is the value of knowing the Key Points to doing a task?
   a. Why is it valuable to know the reasons for the Key Points? In other words, why do we do the task that way?
4. If you were taught jobs using Job Instruction, how well would you say you remember how to do the tasks you were taught?

Part 3 Job Relations

Questions for Leaders (key questions are in bold):

1. **What are the specific goals for the Job Relations program at your organization (e.g., reduce involuntary terminations, decrease turnover, etc.)?**
   a. **Please give some examples of how you are deploying Job Relations to achieve those goals.**
2. **How do you follow up and observe managers and supervisors routinely using and applying good Job Relations skills with their employees?**
   a. **Describe your process for coaching them if they struggle with Job Relations?.**
3. Describe how you measure or track use of Job Relations.
   a. How are these tied to the organization's overall objectives?
   b. How are managers and supervisors made aware of these measures, and how do you know they understand why they are being measured in this way?
   c. What is the effect of this follow-up on their performance?
4. Describe your focus on prevention of problems using the Job Relations Foundations for Good Relations. Give some examples.
5. What would you say are the results or outcomes of the application of Job Relations in the workforce (e.g., improved morale)?
   a. In what ways does this help achieve the overall goals and objectives of the organization?
   b. Please give some examples.
6. What obstacles do you face when using Job Relations to achieve your organizational goals?
   a. Describe how you were able to overcome those obstacles.

7. How do you measure the effectiveness of Job Relations in your organization?
8. Where do you want to be a year from now?

Questions for Managers (key questions are in bold):

1. **Describe how you apply the 4-Step Method for solving people problems on a regular basis.**
   a. **What have been some results?**
   b. **In what ways are relationships with your people improving?**
   c. **Describe how you use or have used the Foundations for Good Job Relations in preventing problems.**
2. Can you share an example of an experience you have had solving a problem using JR?
3. Explain the goals and objectives your organization has for using Job Relations.
   a. How do you apply Job Relations to move the organization toward those goals and objectives?
4. Describe the effect of having a consistent method of leadership across all departments of the organization.
   a. How does that help you achieve goals in your own department?
5. What are some of the obstacles to using the Job Relations method? How are you overcoming them?
   a. Do you think it is worth the effort? Why?
6. How will you sustain the good relations you have built using Job Relations?

Questions for Associates (key questions are in bold):

1. **Describe any changes you have noticed in how your supervisor deals with you since the advent of the Job Relations training at your organization.**
   a. **Please give some examples. In what ways is it beneficial to you?**
   b. **Do you see your relationship with your supervisor improving?**
      i. **In what way?**
2. Does your supervisor regularly communicate with you, getting your opinions and feelings, letting you know how you are doing on your job, and telling you in advance about changes that will affect you?
   a. If so, what effect is that having on your relationship?

3. In what ways does your supervisor give you credit when you do something well?
4. Do you see your supervisor getting into people issues and problems early before they become full-blown 5-alarm fires?
   a. Please give an example.

Part 4 Job Methods

Questions for Leaders (key questions are in bold):

1. **Describe your organization's thinking on continuous improvement.**
   a. **How can or will Job Methods assist in creating a culture of improvement in your organization?**
2. Describe how employee ideas are valued and nurtured in your organization.
   a. What is the approach for bringing out employees' ideas for improvement?
   b. How is it sustained?
3. What is the process for measuring improvements, and how is that tied to the goals and objectives of the organization?
   a. What does that mean (e.g., recognition or reward) for the employees who participate in those improvement activities?
   b. How is the TWI Job Methods program used in this process?
4. Describe the effect on the organization of letting front-line associates participate in improvement activity by giving their ideas and suggestions.
5. How has the TWI Job Methods program helped move the organization toward its goals and objectives?
   a. Please give some examples.
6. How do you measure the effectiveness of Job Methods in your organization?
7. Where do you want to be with JM a year from now?

Questions for Managers (key questions are in bold):

1. **Describe how you have used the Job Methods plan to make improvements in your worksite.**

2. Can you show me a current and proposed breakdown sheet for Job Methods and describe how you got to the improvement proposal?
   a. Explain how the improvement was implemented. What were the results?
3. Can you explain how the JM breakdown connects to the Improvement Kata, idea generation system, etc.?
   a. How are the Kata groups using JM in their Kata activities?
4. What are the advantages of getting your employees involved in the Job Methods analysis and improvement development?
   a. How has this helped with teamwork, morale, engagement, etc.?
5. Describe how your JM practice relates to your Job Instruction and Job Relations activity.
6. Are associates who have not taken the JM 10-hour class allowed to participate in the JM activities?
   a. If so, how has this benefited the improvement activity?

Questions for Associates (key questions are in bold):

1. **Please give examples of how your manager or supervisor regularly asks for your ideas on how to improve Job Methods in your department.**
   a. **How has this changed your view of your job and the organization and how it works?**
2. Describe your experience in working with people in your team on improvement activities.
3. What are your impressions of working with the Job Methods plan?

Appendix 3: Kata Deployment Review Questions

Part 1 Kata Alignment

Questions for Leaders (key questions are in bold):

1. **What does Kata mean to this organization?**
2. **What would you say is Kata's role in promoting the principles and values to which the organization aspires?**
3. **How integral are the Kata routine and thinking pattern skills to achieving the strategic goals and objectives of the organization?**
   a. **Please explain the link between a Kata challenge outcome metrics and strategic A3 initiatives.**
4. **Does this entity have an active Shepherding Group for the Kata teams?**
   a. **What is the purpose of the Shepherding Group?**
5. What does Kata look like at the top leadership levels of this entity?
   a. How is Kata practiced and guided daily by leadership?
6. How often does leadership review and assess the current state of the Improvement Katas and Coaching Katas in relation to each team's challenge?
7. How does leadership handle turnover at the coaching or learner's level for each team's Kata challenge?
8. How do you determine which method of the management system (Kata, TWI, huddle boards, etc.) is used to meet the challenges facing this entity?

    a. Please explain the decision-making process used to determine which areas need a different management system tool/method than Kata to accomplish an objective.

        i. Who is involved in making that decision?

9. How are you spreading Kata to off-shifts and weekends?
10. When a Kata team reaches a challenge or closes a strategic gap, what happens next with that Kata team?
11. How does the leadership celebrate with a Kata team when it achieves victories?

Questions for Directors/Managers (Coaches) (key questions are in bold):

1. **What does Kata look like at your level in this entity?**
    a. **Is it practiced and guided daily by leadership?**
2. How often do you coach a Kata session?
3. How often do you review and assess the current state of the Improvement Kata and Coaching Kata in relation to the strategic initiatives of this entity?
4. Describe the process for setting challenges for your Kata.

Questions for Managers/Supervisors (Learners) (key questions are in bold):

1. **How does your Kata challenge relate to the organization's overall strategic plan?**
2. **Describe the process for setting challenges for your Kata.**

Part 2 Skill Development

Questions for Leaders (Shepherds) (key questions are in bold):

1. **What do the Shepherds do when they go to Coaching Kata cycles?**
    a. **What is their purpose for going to observe a cycle?**
2. **How are learners' and coaches' competencies and skills evaluated?**
3. **Are Shepherds involved in evaluating the competency of learners, Kata coaches, and kata 2nd coaches? Please explain.**
4. Which leaders are also Kata Shepherds?
5. Describe the path to become a Shephard in the Coaching Kata structure.

6. Is there a certain minimum time required as a Kata coach before some-one can become a Shepherd?
7. How often do Shepherds attend a Coaching Kata cycle for which they Shepherd?
8. How does this entity evaluate peoples' Kata skill development?
   a. How many learners do you have at this entity?
   b. How many competent learners do you have at this entity?
   c. How many Kata coaches do you have at this entity?
   d. How many competent Kata coaches and competent Kata 2nd coaches do you have at this entity?
   e. Please explain the process for assessing a learner's skill sets and the frequency of such assessments.
   f. Please explain the process for assessing a Kata coach's skill sets and the frequency of such assessments.
   g. What would indicate to you that a learner is ready to be a Kata coach?
   h. What would indicate to you that a Kata coach is ready to be a Kata 2nd coach?

Questions for Managers (Coaches) (key questions are in bold):

1. **Are Shepherds involved in evaluating the competency of learners, Kata coaches, and Kata 2nd coaches? Please explain.**
2. **How does this entity evaluate peoples' Kata skill development?**
   a. **How many learners do you have at this entity?**
   b. **How many competent learners do you have at this entity?**
   c. **How many Kata coaches do you have at this entity?**
   d. **How many competent Kata coaches and competent Kata 2nd coaches do you have at this entity?**
   e. **Please explain the process for assessing a learner's skill sets and the frequency of such assessments.**
   f. **Please explain the process for assessing a Kata coach's skill sets and the frequency of such assessments.**
   g. **What would indicate to you that a learner is ready to be a Kata coach?**
   h. **What would indicate to you that a Kata coach is ready to be a Kata 2nd coach?**

Part 3 Quality Storyboard Structure and Alignment

Questions for Leaders (2nd Coaches & Shepherds) (key questions are in bold):
Questions for Managers & Supervisors (Learners & 1st Coaches) (key questions are in bold):

1. **How can you tell if a Kata storyboard is of high quality or low quality?**
   a. **Please describe a high-quality Kata storyboard.**
   b. **Please describe a low-quality Kata storyboard.**
2. **Can you explain the significance and key points of this quality storyboard standard (shown in Figure 5.3)? What are the key relationships between each of the areas and their relationship with the overall direction of the Kata?**
   a. **Assessors: Use large printout of the quality storyboard to record answers during the interview.**
3. Watch the YouTube video called, "Improvement Kata Learner's Storyboard Content and Connections."
4. Please take me to some of your storyboards so that we can compare them to the quality storyboard standard.
   a. How do these storyboards match the quality storyboard standard?
   b. If any parts of your storyboard don't match, what impact do you think that is having on your success with this Kata challenge?

Part 4 Obstacles

Questions for Managers & Supervisors (Learners & 1st Coaches) (key questions are in bold):

1. **How would you describe or define an obstacle?**
2. **How are obstacles to the target condition found?**
   a. **How are the extended team of process owners (the staff and workers) involved in determining obstacles?**
3. How are obstacles prioritized based on their impact on the target condition?
   a. Are learners free to choose the "one" obstacle they would like to work on, even if it may not seem to be a high priority? Explain.

4. What components should a 1st coach look for as a learner writes and describes an obstacle?
5. Please explain how the "one" obstacle selected by the learner is causing a barrier to this target condition?
6. What is the importance or significance of the "How will you measure that?" column for each obstacle?
7. How can you tell if the learner is actively working through the obstacles via PDSAs and learnings from PDSAs?

Part 5 The Improvement Coaching Kata

Questions for Leaders (Shepherds) (key questions are in bold):
Questions for Managers & Supervisors (Learners & Kata Coaches) (key questions are in bold):

1. **Please demonstrate a Kata Coach-Learner 5Q Kata for a challenge in this area and tell me the Improvement Kata and Coaching Kata experience level (skill level and length of time) of the learner and Kata coach.**
2. **Please demonstrate a Kata 2nd coach – Kata coach Coaching Kata for the coaching cycle we just witnessed. Tell me the experience level (skill level and length of time) of the learner and coaches.**

Part 6 The Improvement Kata and Coaching Kata Routine

Questions for Learners and 1st Coaches (key questions are in bold):

1. **Which type of experiment is the last PDSA step? What makes it that type?**
2. **Did the last step get you closer to the target condition? If so, how can you tell?**
3. **What do you see that could have made this last PDSA experiment better or more impactful?**
4. Which type of experiment is the next PDSA step? What makes it that type?
5. Please explain how completing this next PDSA step will get you closer to the target condition.

6. Is there anything you see that could make the next PDSA experiment better or more impactful?
7. Does this next PDSA step build off the last PDSA step? If so, can you explain to me how you can tell?
8. In the last PDSA step, has the learner deeply reflected on what s/he has learned? What indicates this?
9. Does this next PDSA step address the one obstacle the learner just told us about? If so, please explain how the PDSA experiment will address the obstacle.
10. What does the term "threshold of knowledge" mean to you?
11. In this last PDSA experiment, did the learner work at the edge of the threshold of knowledge? What indicates to you that s/he is or is not at the edge of the threshold of knowledge?
12. In this next PDSA experiment, is the learner working at the edge of the threshold of knowledge? What indicates to you that s/he is or is not at the edge of the threshold of knowledge?

Part 7 2nd Coaching Cycle

Questions for 2nd Coaches (key questions are in bold):

1. **What was the Kata coach striving to achieve with the learner in this Coaching Kata cycle?**
2. **Please help me understand how you think this Coaching Kata cycle went.**
   a. **Please expand beyond "good" or "It went well."**
3. **Did the learner address what you were striving to achieve from this Coaching Kata cycle?**
   a. **If yes, please help me understand how the learner addressed it.**
   b. **If no, please help me understand how the learner did not address it.**
4. **What type of experiment is this, and how can you tell?**
5. **How will you know when this selected obstacle (or any of the other obstacles) is overcome permanently?**
6. **What would indicate to you that this learner is ready to start a Kata storyboard or be a Kata coach?**

7. Are the obstacles to this target condition being measured and tracked?

   a. If so, how have you been measuring and tracking these obstacles?

8. What is the skill level of this learner that just practiced the Improvement Kata for this challenge?

9. What is the skill level of this Kata coach that just practiced the Coaching Kata for this challenge?

10. What happens with the Coaching Kata routine when your learner has not completed the last PDSA step when you arrive to start the session?

11. Attendance:

    a. How do you track the frequency and attendance of these Coaching Kata routines?

    b. What happens when the learner of a Kata team is absent 1–2 days?

    c. What happens if the learner is off on PTO for an extended period of a week or two?

    d. What happens when the Kata coach of a Kata team is absent 1–2 days?

12. Resetting Kata Trajectory Components:

    a. What indicates to you that a target condition has been reached?

    b. Is reaching the outcome metric(s) the main factor – meaning we have achieved the outcome metric(s), so it is time to reset the Target Condition?

    c. Please describe how you think about or go about resetting a target condition once it is reached or the achieve-by date comes?

       i. Help me understand what that process looks like.

    d. What indicates to you that a challenge has been reached?

    e. Is reaching the outcome metric(s) the main factor, meaning we have achieved the outcome metric(s), so the challenge is met?

    f. How long must the team's performance be sustained before you determine that the challenge level of performance is sustainable?

       i. What happens to the Kata team next?

    g. If the achieve-by date or challenge due date comes and the Kata team has not fully reached the challenge condition state, what happens to the Kata team next?

    h. Please describe how you think about or go about resetting a challenge once a Challenge is reached before the achieve-by date comes.

       i. Help me understand what that process looks like.

Questions for Shepherds (key questions are in bold):

1. **How does this area's challenge link to the strategic initiatives of this entity?**
2. **Do the outcome metric(s) on this Kata storyboard and Coaching Kata just demonstrated match or support the challenge metric and ultimately a strategic goal for this entity?**
   a. **If so, please describe the linkage.**
3. **How do you know if a team is struggling?**
4. What skill level is the Kata coach that just practiced the Coaching Kata for this challenge?
5. What does the process look like for assessing skill of this Kata coach?
6. What obstacles are you facing with this Kata coach's skill development?
7. How often does the target condition for this Kata storyboard get reset? How do the Kata coach and learner reflect on previous target conditions?
8. Help me understand who determines if the target condition has been met and how that decision is made, to make a change in focus process for this Kata challenge.
9. What would indicate to you that this Kata coach is ready to be a Kata 2nd coach?
10. What would indicate to you that this Kata 2nd coach is ready to coach multiple Kata storyboards?
11. How often do this learner, Kata coach, and Kata 2nd coach meet in front of this storyboard for a coaching Kata cycle?
12. What have you observed the Kata 2nd coach do upon making an observation?
    a. How often do you, the Shepherd of this Kata, attend a Coaching Kata cycle in front of this storyboard with learner, Kata coach, and Kata 2nd coach?
    b. What does the Shepherd do when he/she makes an observation?

Index

Locators in *italics* refer to Tables and Figures; those in **bold** refer to text boxes. Footnotes are denoted by n, e.g. 6n2. Abbreviations: TWI = Training Within Industry.